Evangelization or Colonization?

Series Preface

The **Global Voices** series takes the missiological work of writers who have written in their own language and makes this accessible to the English-speaking world through translation and republishing. The key principle here is that the translated work reflects the context, experience and thinking of the local context. In so doing, Regnum Books seeks to amplify voices less easily heard outside their own contexts. Work of this nature will make a significant contribution to the development of 'polycentric missiology'; namely, mission thinking and practice that truly reflects the contexts, concerns and contributions of the global church in all its rich diversity.

Series Editors

Paul Bendor-Samuel	Executive Director, Oxford Centre for Mission Studies
Mark Greenwood	BMS Overseas Team Leader for South America and Sub-Saharan Africa
Timóteo Carriker	Mission educator and consultant to the Brazilian Bible Society

REGNUM GLOBAL THEOLOGICAL VOICES

Evangelization or Colonization?

Analzira Nascimento

Translated by John Clark, David Grainger and Elídia Grainger
from the original in Portuguese

First published 2021 by Regnum Books International
Originally published in Portuguese by: Editora Ultimato Ltda, 2015
ISBN: 978-85-7779-117-0

Regnum is an imprint of the Oxford Centre for Mission Studies
St. Philip and St. James Church
Woodstock Road
Oxford OX2 6HR, UK
www.ocms.ac.uk/regnum

09 08 07 06 05 04 03 7 6 5 4 3 2 1

British Library Cataloguing in Publication Data
A catalogue record for this book is available from the British Library

ISBN: 978-1-5064-8900-1
eBook ISBN: 978-1-5064-8901-8

Typeset by Words by Design

*The texts of the Biblical references were taken from the New International Version,
(International Bible Society), unless otherwise specified.*

The publication of this volume is made possible through the
financial assistance of **Evangelisches Missionswerk**
and **BMS World Mission.**

Distributed by 1517 Media in the US, Canada, India, and Brazil

Contents

Preface

During the course of history, the Church has adopted evangelizing practices that have contributed towards forming the basis of a model of mission strongly marked by the ideals of the enterprises of colonial expansion in the late 15th and early 16th centuries. This model was formed in the United States, influenced by Puritanism and Pietism, with the refinement of Enlightenment ideas, and gave rise to the dominant Protestant missionary format today.

In the present day, the Church, in its encounters with 'the other', zealous in its pursuit of expansion programmes, continues to replicate the same colonialist logic of domination, which, by definition, reinforces the denial of the identity of 'the other'.

This book was elaborated from the doctoral thesis *Missão e Alteridade – decolonizar o paradigma missiológico,* [Mission and Otherness – decolonizing the missiological paradigm] which problematizes this missionary standard. It aims to contribute to the ideas of those who are uncomfortable with our models, that they may dare to think that new "ways of doing" are possible. Gradually (hopefully) one can deconstruct what has been produced by the tradition of mission as it has been shaped by historical needs, and can return to the simple and incarnational model of our Lord and Master Jesus, the Christ of God. It proposes a way back where the focus is to work and to live *with* 'the other', not *for* them.

I hope that this reading will be useful to those who are concerned about God's purpose for the planet and how their life mission can co-operate with what God is doing in the world.

Analzira Nascimento
December 2014

Introduction

In 1985, I went to work in Angola, Africa, where I stayed for seventeen years. From the outset, I could verify that the missionary model that reigned in Brazil and which sent me to Angola could no longer provide answers to the new challenges that were emerging in the world, much less to the local demands that I faced in my daily routines.

Suddenly, I found myself in a rather strange universe: living in a new culture, which was quite different from the Western one and had been radically changed by two wars,[1] a centralizing government of the Marxist-Leninist sort, and living in a city that was the epicentre of armed conflict, isolated at certain periods by fighting.

After numerous difficulties trying to adapt and some cultural errors, only reasons beyond my control prevented me returning to Brazil. However, my training in nursing gave me a new chance and guided my missionary project to that nation, giving a new direction to my life. This is how our team, suffering with the Angolan church, decided not to be held hostage by the situation, nor succumb to the misery that was imposed by war and its ramifications. Together, we organized the "counter-attack", we resisted and discovered that the crisis brought unmissable opportunities for the church to carry out its mission.

Our venture of reappraising motives, meaning, objectives and goals led me to "reinvent" my programme of work, principally with the resurgence of the political-military conflict that had ravaged the whole country. New questions required new responses, leading us to focus our actions on producing agents of change and, with local leaders, working towards the transformation of realities by means of development projects, as I have proposed in another work.[2] There was a fruitful exchange with international organizations and several socio-missionary projects were implemented, generating jobs and income which restored dignity and self-esteem to the people and contributed to the city's development.

This forced my missionary practice into the process of "daily doing", of sacrificial service, negotiating constantly and recognizing our interdependence and, as much as possible, working for the construction of a better society.

In August 2002, I was invited by the Board of Missions of the Brazilian Baptist Convention to return to Brazil to work with the formation of missionaries and to co-ordinate the Volunteers Without Frontiers Project whose purpose is to prepare and send youth teams to countries with low indices of human development (HDI), mainly in Africa. The initial pedagogical plan focused on mission programmes, engaging in social transformation projects. The "laboratory" in Angola had already demonstrated that the transformation of communities by the integral gospel was possible, and therefore it was fundamental to review our model of mission, which, according to David Bosch, cannot be restricted to the preaching of the gospel, but must constitute a multifaceted ministry.[3] For him, the definition of mission overlaps with the understanding of what the Church was called to perform in the world.

To develop an innovative programme facing attacks of a theology of maintenance was, therefore, what challenged me to begin to work on the research culminating in writing this book. Delving into different tendencies and currents of thought in the present-day missionary movement, I have perceived and discovered evidence that my concern – which initially seems to have been limited to the scope of strategies and methodologies in relation to this mismatch – was not only relevant to Baptist operational questions, but that Protestant Brazil, in general, has reproduced a model inspired by a vision of the world that was showing clear signs of exhaustion. The investigation has led me to new possibilities and my understanding has taken on other directions, helping me to understand that the problem was not simply restricted to a need to review "the ways of doing things". Co-existence with other evangelical groups has made a contribution to the delimitation of my thesis. I was still intrigued by the question of why some sincere and well-meaning Christians, concerned with the spiritual situation or even with all the aspects of human life, continue to reproduce a missionary practice characterized as "the superiors who know and can solve the problems of 'the other' and decide that which is good for them"; why even some advocates of a discourse that calls on the contemporary church to insert itself better in society and to educate their eyes towards an interpretation differentiated in terms of challenges beyond its gates cannot manage to build a dialogical relationship and escape the imperialist methods in their encounters with each other.

My hypothesis is that, in encounters with 'the other', in the eagerness to fulfil an ecclesiastical agenda, the missionary often fails to recognize oneself as a subject. The mission model which predominates, especially in the evangelical world, continues reproducing the same Eurocentric colonialist logic of domination, which in its vertical approach reinforces the denial of the identity of 'the other' and reduces it to an object.

My proposal is to provoke a reflection around a theme of otherness that presupposes, in social relationships, the identification of what 'the other' is. Humans interact, are interdependent; however, 'the other' is a distinct being and their subjectivity must be preserved, in opposition to the "banking"[4] approach which prioritizes depositing content into people, especially those who live "outside the Christian camp".

David Bosch's theses on the missionary project throughout history have helped to advance my ideas. He argues that the mission paradigm was strongly contaminated by its origin in Western colonialism and that it must cease to be a symbol of the universality of Western imperialism.[5]

This book is organized into four chapters. Chapter one introduces the paradigmatic socio-cultural and epistemological crisis that we are experiencing at the beginning of the millennium, which also has affected the Christian missionary project. According to Boaventura de Sousa Santos, we are in a period of paradigmatic transition that is characterized by a time of search, not for new knowledge, but for a new way of producing knowledge. He encourages us to have a critical attitude toward Western Reason, which has been reigning from the Enlightenment, "a rationality that dominates in the North and which has had a huge influence on all our ways of thinking, our sciences, our conceptions of life and of the world".[6] It is an "indolent reason" because it considers itself unique and does not want to see the epistemological diversity and the wealth of other cultures. It produces monocultures that cover the others and make them invisible because they are different and do not fit into its hegemonic conception of reality.

In chapter one, I try to show how much the Enlightenment influenced thought and the missionary practice, configuring the feeling of Western superiority that was strengthened by the colonialist projects. Today this model of missionary action has entered into a time of crisis and needs to acquire the capability to overcome its mismatch with our new world, which values and respects cultural diversity.

Chapter two gives a retrospective on the history of Christianity focusing not on accounts of major events but on the concept of Christianity since the 4th century, to show how the mission model was being based on the understanding of the Church's role in the world through each era. It shows how the Iberian project through colonialist undertakings in the conquest of America was determinant in delineating the current model of missionary practice.

Arriving at the 16th century, chapter three explores the other side of the fork in the road in the history of Christianity, which begins with the Protestant Reformation, and gives rise to a new model, and yet to a project which is also imperialist and monocultural. With marks of Puritanism and Pietism, this model is formatted in the United States, becoming a matrix for the dominant missionary paradigm.

In chapter four, I propose a re-encounter with a dialogical missionary action to obey a new decolonialized logic. In order to escape the current coloniality, I defend the recovery of the ideal biblical model, learning from history and the education of the gaze which sees the world in the perspective of 'the other'. I emphasize the importance of escaping from every colonialization of Christian approaches, which, as Boaventura de Sousa Santos says, "is nothing less than the inability to establish relationship with 'the other', but to transform it into an object."[7] It is necessary to stop invading "the other's house", understand that 'the other' also has something to say and that, in hearing, we will achieve conditions of dialogue.

1. Paradigmatic Crisis:
The Exhaustion of Western Models

We are living through a period of transition marked by major socio-political and cultural changes, both globally and locally. We are observing the exhaustion of models which were points of reference and determined the ways of thinking and doing. At the threshold of this new emergent world which is suffocating the previous one, making it obsolete, there are crises arising not only from the inadequacy of new realities, but also from the presence of different worldviews that co-exist simultaneously in different moments of each society, generating mismatches between the conservative and the emergent. Some critics have already identified our days as a period of paradigmatic crisis.

These phenomena have been changing our points of reference and leading us towards new ways of understanding reality and have unfolded in the most varied segments of society, reaching the Christian world in a certain way, in particular the missionary model.

Our society has changed considerably, and the Church has continued with the same discourse as addressed to a population of past decades. Its practice follows a methodology that, in education, Paulo Freire calls "banking education",[1] where the student is simply a container where the contents of that education are deposited. Their posture is passive, where it is enough to just memorize and regurgitate information. There is no dialogical relationship, the educational action "becomes an act of depositing, in which the students are the depositaries and the educator, the depositor".

The missionary activity of the Church, which enables dialogue with the world outside the ecclesiastical reality, is also facing an unprecedented mismatch. If we apply "banking education" to missionary practice, the student would be 'the other', the object or depositary of missionary practice, and the educator is the missionary, the depositor, who holds the knowledge and therefore ignores or does not consider what local people already know. This practice can no longer be imposed. It tries to give answers to questions that are no longer being asked.

The Socio-Cultural Paradigmatic Crisis

In defending his thesis on the paradigmatic transition, Boaventura de Sousa Santos argued that the Western epistemological paradigm, which has dominated for many years, has increasingly been showing signs of exhaustion and no longer reflecting scientific practice. It is already possible to conclude that "science in general and not only the social sciences were based on an epistemological paradigm and a model of rationality that gave signs of exhaustion, signs so evident that we could speak of a paradigmatic crisis."[2]

He states that the cause of our condition is because we are in a transition period, that is, we have modern problems for which we have no modern solutions. And this gives our time the character of transition. It is a crisis of hegemonic thinking arising from Eurocentric reason. It is indolent, because it refuses to see other knowledge, seek new solutions, and is unable to produce new ideas. This bankruptcy, which is becoming increasingly visible, is also the great challenge for working for the construction of an emerging model, still difficult to identify.

In another text, he works this theme of the paradigmatic crisis with more specificity, not always related to periods of macro- but also micro-changes. According to him, there are basically two types of paradigmatic crisis: *crises of growth*, when there is dissatisfaction with methods or concepts, which happen most frequently; and *crises of degeneracy*, which involve the whole paradigm and take longer to develop.

Thomas Kuhn, a theoretical physicist, who in the course of his research became very interested in the history of science and philosophy, developed a hypothesis on crises and changes in paradigms. Although Kuhn's theory is restricted to the natural sciences, we can make use of its research and some of the concepts present within it as a working hypothesis, especially since its ideas about the process of model substitution and assimilation can be adapted to the social sciences. According to Kuhn, the new paradigm can emerge – at least in embryonic form – before a crisis is well established or has even been widely recognized, and "considerable time passes between the first awareness of the failure of the paradigm and the emergency of a new one".[3]

Generally, only a few individuals in a group can perceive reality in a qualitatively different way from their contemporaries and predecessors and, in this way, they confirm that the models used can no longer respond to the problems faced. Kuhn comments that, during the period in which the crisis is taking shape, there is a "malfunction", which can be applied to both the scientific and political development. He traces a parallel between political revolutions and scientific revolutions, highlighting in both cases a shared feeling of inadequacy, mismatch, and yearning for answers.

In writing about the origins of the changes, Kuhn stresses that a consciousness of anomaly needs to arise, and this awareness "inaugurates a period in which the categories of conceptual changes are adapted until what was initially considered anomaly becomes predicted".[4] There is a claim that the current models can no longer respond to the problems that arise. However, the transition to a new model will be a period of crisis, characterized as a process of deconstruction of traditions and construction of other models.

However, that which is new does not establish itself easily, since it is more comfortable and safer to work with that which is usual and planned, ignoring the new problems that accumulate, than to admit failure. It is precisely here that we meet the positive aspect of the crisis: the cumulative effect, which may surprise us every moment, also urges us to admit that we are overcome and pushes us to be open to the new – to recognize that the time has come to renew the instruments. Crises offer the community opportunities for confrontation, making new choices possible and are needed in order for the new systems to emerge.

Kuhn suggests that the crisis may end in different ways and enumerates three possibilities, which are pertinent questions to be analysed by those of us judged to be ambassadors for the kingdom of God in this world: 1) the problem may resist even new, seemingly radical approaches; 2) the end of the crisis can occur when normal science proves capable of dealing with the problem; 3) or the crisis can be resolved with the emergence of a new candidate for a paradigm and a subsequent battle for its acceptance.

David Bosch, basing his theory on Kuhn's ideas, used some of the same concepts to defend his thesis about the crisis and the transition paradigm within mission. Commenting on the replacement of models, he argues that in the natural sciences the new model replaces the old in a definitive and irreversible way. However, in the humanities, the two can walk together for a long time, and in the case of theology, it is possible to encounter different lines and trends co-existing simultaneously in distinct periods of history. Nowadays, for example, in several Christian groups it is possible to observe followers of Jesus Christ belonging to the same religious denomination, and yet with very different inclinations, such as fundamentalists, conservatives, liberals and others. In his research on paradigms in history, he concludes that in the field of religion a change of paradigm always means continuity and change, fidelity to the past and courage to face the future.

For the author, the different periods of history, with their particular contexts, have considerably affected Christians' comprehension of biblical faith and consequently, of Christian mission. Bosch also defends the concept of paradigm in the sense of "models of interpretation", since, according to him, our views always constitute mere interpretations of what we consider to be divine revelation. This personal understanding of revelation can also be conditioned by various factors, among them ecclesiastical tradition, context, social position, and the personality and culture of the person.

The initial reflection based on the authors mentioned so far allows us to affirm that both in theology and in science, there is a close relationship between paradigm shift and different perceptions of the world. This is how new patterns of interpretation emerge when a small group or segment or society perceives that existing models are unable to solve problems. Then there is a search for a new theoretical model or structure that responds better to the challenges of the moment.

These new points of reference are not decided or invented by a group or some individual proposal. As the dominant model becomes incompatible with new realities, the new one infiltrates and imposes itself, until it finally conquers the space.

Defenders of dominant models tend to resist new proposals because the change usually compromises their life project. With the new one comes a "redefinition of problems and inconsistencies hitherto unsolvable and gives them a convincing solution; it is on this basis that the scientific community imposes itself. But the replacement of the paradigm is not quick".[5]

The people who espouse the old model, "often, simply cannot understand the arguments of those proposing the new. Speaking metaphorically, on the same board, one is playing chess and the other is playing draughts".[6] The depletion of paradigms, which affects society and culture with a domino effect, and can also provoke mutations in our theoretical structures as is well discussed by Michel de Certeau in his book *Culture in the Plural*. For him, this crisis that reaches our models points to a collapse of ideologies, and the refusal to accept that we are outdated in our way of producing knowledge. That our official maps are collapsing is illustrated by the author as "two forms of unconsciousness": one that refuses to see the wreckage and therefore, denies the problem; and the other that exempts itself from rebuilding, that is, its decision is to give up seeking a solution.[7]

Commenting on this "erosion" in institutions, de Certeau points to the inversion of goals that have been occurring in many organizations, in which striving for survival has become a higher goal than their mission. Sustaining traditions seems more important than searching for their original meaning. For the thinker, it is no longer acceptable to "declare something legitimate because it preserves a power", because the erosion of convictions, and discredit in authorities, which are revealed in the questioning of dogmas and paradigms, are inevitable.

As an example of being attentive to the signs of the times, he cites the vision of Ezekiel in the Old Testament (Ez. 10-11). The Spirit had emigrated with the people exiled to Babylon, leaving the city. Now there are only memories left of a glorious past, a situation described by him as *liturgies* of *absence*, "for he is in another place. He has not failed. He is missing [...] the meaning of the building of the institutions [...] only stones remained".[8] The past has its importance and its value, but we must recognize when the model is exhausted and not allow stagnation, a result of the need to reinforce positions and to "revere relics".

De Certeau spares no criticism of continuity, uniformity, or the linear method of interpreting history – an epistemology which, according to him, governs in silence the profession of the historian. This nonconformity of his reveals and searches for an understanding of human beings in the world in which they are located. Continuity, in addition to hindering creativity and innovation, suffers from the temptation to uniformization. The possibility of change brings insecurity, since the comfort of maintenance is better than the risk of the unknown and the new. However, the reaction to changes may bring some dangers: total rupture with the past and denial of any continuity, or resistance to armoured positions and lack of humility for reflection discussion in the face of the new. For de Certeau, true modernity brings recognition of diversity, but intransigence, uniformity and dogmatism are manifestations of the medieval model that we inherited and which still influences our way of thinking.

Discussing changes in society and transition processes, Zygmunt Bauman develops the concepts of "liquidity", "solidity" and "fluidity" as appropriate metaphors for understanding the new. The term "melt the solids" in the text is used to describe the phenomena that attack the "freezing" of established standards and those agreed by the present system as normative, triggering new changes and generating changes in the frames of reference. Opting for tradition and resisting "liquefaction" promotes continuity that leads to inflexibility to accept new ways of thinking-doing; nevertheless, the author warns us of the dangers of this endeavour in the construction of a new order. Caution is needed in demolitions and removal of the "debris"! The fear of change causes stagnation, as the preoccupation to "maintain" positions exceeds the openness to reflect on motivations and correct methods.

Change brings risks because, before it reaches the *status* of normality, it fights true battles with conservatism, which fights for the preservation of traditional values. However, the clash between different worldviews becomes predictable in the transitional phase, and the journey towards a crystallization of the new way of understanding or doing can be lengthy.

The exhaustion of models, and attempts to understand changes to society for definitions of new "interpretation lenses", is a subject widely debated by Touraine in his book *New Paradigm: for understanding today's world* which describes how the late Middle Ages accelerated the disappearance of the religious order in the world and replaced it with the political order. Centuries later, the Industrial Revolution and Capitalism emerge as milestones for a new moment in history, thus signalling a triumph of the economic and social model over the political model. However, in the 21st century, we can perceive that these social categories are insufficient to explain the cultural phenomena which we see in the present world and which cannot give the answers we hope for. We feel the rupture more and more. We contemplate cultural categories rapidly substituting social categories because "we are changing paradigm in our representation of collective and personal life. We are leaving the era in which everything was expressed and explained in social terms and we need to define in what terms this new paradigm is built".[9]

Touraine clearly makes his goal to show the end of a world and the transition to a different one. We have moved from social movements to cultural movements, a process he also calls the "decomposition of the social paradigm". This social crisis is generating an individualistic universe capable of producing a new direction and a life expectancy which social and political institutions find it difficult to manage.

Another contribution to the worsening of the current situation was savage capitalism which encouraged the race for consumption and accumulation of goods, generating a market culture which values human beings for what they have and not for what they are, and which went on to reinforce and further provoke the definition of the outline of a crisis.

This search for meaning and disenchantment with institutions and values of Western culture, in turn, are bringing "A new sensitivity to the world as a whole which is generating new values, dreams and behaviours".[10] Enrique Dussel develops the concept of "trans-modernity" to refer to a global liberation project, which includes the peripheral world and in which the otherness is realized equally (solidarity of the centre with the periphery), that is, for a global decolonial model. These scholars of the Postcolonial Theory, also called "Decolonial Studies", maintain that a perception of the unequal relationships between North and South provides an understanding of or an explanation for the contemporary world, and, for them, these "relations were historically constituted by colonialism and the end of colonialism as a political relationship did not bring about the end of colonialism as a social relation, as a mentality and form of authoritarian and discriminatory sociability".[11]

In speaking about the recognition of diversity and dialogue of cultures, Boaventura warns us about the dangers of falling into the trap of standardization, as well as the importance of remembering that "hegemony is an attempt to create consensus based on the idea that what it produces is good for everyone".[12] The recognition of diversity and plurality is fundamental in intercultural dialogue.

Paulo Suess, when writing about the meetings between different cultures throughout history, shows how our concepts and also our practices, including the missionary ones, can mutate in these contacts because "theory and praxis – the truths of faith as much as the pastoral practices – always 'suffer' the interference of cultural and historical mediations".[13]

For missiology[14], there is a reflection and a warning to learn from history, not only valuing good experiences, but also having the humility to recognize in this that the evolution of the emergent ideas are often linked to the lack of answers and lack of confidence in the established paradigm. Comparing the current missionary model with the new possibilities that are emerging, we realize that it is possible to reflect from a Southern Hemisphere perspective, whilst accepting the challenge of working in a counter-hegemonic form that can overcome the dominant matrix.

The Paradigmatic Crisis in Missionary Practice

The paradigmatic crisis that has taken a hold in our time also has affected the Church and its missionary enterprise. The enlightenment paradigm, which from the 17th century settled in the sciences, also contaminated theology with its influence contributing to consolidate a Christian conception of 'the other' that was already previously impregnated with the logic of colonialist expansion movements and would now define the type approach used in this encounter with the unknown and the different in missionary action.

David Bosch, in his book *Transforming Mission: Paradigm Shifts in Theology of Mission*, undertook research analysing the different models of mission throughout the history of the Church and finished his work giving the "contours" of a new missionary paradigm. However, in his conclusion, he limits himself to reveal some "elements of this supposed emerging paradigm". He makes a diagnosis of the current state of mission, a synthesis of his main thesis, affirming categorically that "the missionary enterprise in modern society in its entirety is so contaminated by its origins in Western colonialism and its close association with it, which is irremediable; we have to find a completely new image today".[15]

In this work, he also endeavoured to demonstrate how socio-political changes can lead to reflection and the need to review methods of action in various sectors of society, stating that we live in a time of transition, in the border area between a model which no longer satisfies and another which is still hazy. Periods of change are generally characterized by a time of crisis. When analysing the models that marked the different periods of history, he affirms that each one constitutes the end of one world and the birth of another. We live on the threshold between the old and the new model, identified as a period of uncertainties and crises.

Bosch divided the history of Christianity into six major paradigms. He gave a historical retrospective of the missionary, mapping the sociocultural panorama of each period, outlining the trends and how the Church interpreted the world of its time: the apocalyptic model of early Christianity, the missionary model of the Eastern Church, the missionary model of the medieval Roman Catholic Church, the missionary model of the Protestant Reformation, the modern model of the Enlightenment and, finally, in the contemporary world, the search for an emerging model.

Describing the paradigms of mission in the history of Christianity, the author argues that in periods of great changes there is always a crisis arising from the process of adaptation and change. It would be what he calls "creative tension" between the new and the old.

One of David Bosch's opponents asks if he would have managed to "build" a new paradigm if his death had not interrupted his research. In his book *Paradigms in Conflict*, David Hesselgrave, a conservative missiologist, admits the paradigm crisis, but does not accept innovative ideas and gets stuck in the model that only discusses ways to propagate the call of the "Great Commission" – the last command given by Jesus Christ to his church to go and make disciples. According to him, what is fascinating and at the same time frustrating is that "Bosch provokes us by suggesting that a variety of paradigms could be constructed through his critical hermeneutics. However, he himself never builds even a single paradigm".[16]

Another critic of Bosch's studies, Alan Kreider, disagrees with the elaborate division in which Bosch identifies six model periods of mission and defends only three: pre-Christendom, Christianity and post-Christendom.[17] However, he states that the model proposed by Bosch, the emerging ecumenical or postmodern, is probably the same as that suggested by him, or it is also implicitly a "post-Christendom" model. Kreider comments in his text that some European theologians are even writing about the "mission after Christendom".

Bosch presents all the contours of the Enlightenment worldview and how this perception contaminated missionary thought, emphasizing belief in the victory of progress, because it was believed that Westerners would solve the problems of the world. This premise of the superiority of reason reigned for centuries. The idea of the emancipated and autonomous individual predominated and there was no place for God. The strictly Enlightenment separation between subject and object in the natural sciences was also applied to theology. The dominion over nature and its objectification and subjection of the physical world to the human mind and will had disastrous consequences, including the worsening of ecological imbalance that plagues the world today.

Bosch's position is that the Enlightenment also reduced the once so wide range of interests of the Church for life and society as a whole. He supports the idea that, only years later, people "touched" by the *Awakening*, that is, by the movements of revivals,[18] began to pity the poor and the excluded again.

These ideas of progress and superiority nourished by the Enlightenment encouraged the conquistadors to venture in search of domains, for it was "largely Enlightenment oriented by progress which had engendered the project of colonial expansion".[19]

An American belief grounded in and enriched by the Enlightenment worldview was that of Manifest Destiny, the result of strong nationalism, rooted in belief in the superiority of Western countries and with a strong tendency to treat other cultures as inferior. It reached its maximum expression in the colonial expansion of the West and was considered to be the apogee of colonialism. The Americans believed that God chose them, because of their qualities, to be his representatives before other peoples. Not only did the "civilized" feel superior to the "uncivilized" but also responsible for them. Although we are aware of various missionary works with sincere motivations, we must also recognize that in wake of this followed the Western missionary enterprise, which in this period started not only with the premise of the superiority of western culture, but also the conviction that God, in his providence, had chosen the nations of the West, based on their unique qualities, to be standard-bearers for his cause, around the world.[20]

We must admit that some missionary movements were partners and accomplices in these imperialist ethnocentric programmes which led to the annihilation of indigenous cultures. The mission and colonization were interdependent projects. The Enlightenment culture, largely responsible for the Western conception of knowledge and rationality, printed its matrix in the sciences and strengthened a sense of superiority such that Westerners felt more rational than other people.

The Church could not break with this logic and model and the words of the author only confirm that the missionary movement of the last three centuries has emerged from this matrix:

> It was inevitable that the Enlightenment would profoundly influence missionary thinking and practice, especially if we consider that the whole modern missionary undertaking is, to a very significant degree, a product of the Enlightenment. After all, it was an expansionist worldview that broadened the horizons of Europe beyond the Mediterranean and the Atlantic and thus prepared the way for the worldwide expansion of the Christian mission.[21]

Bosch, in addition to blaming the Enlightenment for the Western epistemological hegemony, in which other forms of knowledge were not only not respected but also downgraded, further strengthens our realization that the Western missionary movement was strongly influenced by the Enlightenment.

Within this framework and starting with it, the "forces of renewal" emerge with spiritual revivals as attempts at resistance to Enlightenment ideas. They gave a new impulse to the modern missionary movement, although predominantly the modern missions had their origin in the environment of modern Western colonialism, in complicity with colonial powers.

Tzvetan Todorov, in his book *The Conquest of America: the question of the other*, also delves into these questions of domination and power, when he addresses the theme of alterability and monoculturalism striving to demonstrate the real intentions of the "discoverers", especially the crusading ideals of Columbus. He denounces the complicity of the Church, both Catholic and Protestant sides, in these hegemonic movements of colonization, pointing out their participation in real cultural damage. Undoubtedly, these acts compromised their missionary practice, because "in both cases it denies the identity of the other; whether on the plane of existence, as in the case of Catholics; or on the plane of values, like Protestants; it is a somewhat derisory to try to know which team is the record holder on the way to the destruction of the other".[22]

The accounts of explorers and merchants such as Marco Polo and Columbus, although principal figures of different times, show that the maritime enterprises, beyond the desire to find riches, expressed the motives of the Crusade movement. Todorov and Dussel point out, for example, hegemonic intentions of the rulers of Spain, who only invested in voyages expecting big profits, and the aim of the navigator Columbus: to arrive in the Indies and to enable the expansion of Christianity. This became an obsession; he died in 1506 "with the clear 'awareness' of having discovered the way from the West to Asia".[23]

His tireless pursuit of gold on at least three trips is explained as this would represent the recognition of his pioneering. According to Todorov, after having studied several letters organized by Bartolomeu de Las Casas,[24] returning with riches would validate the investment by the kings into his voyages and further nourish the ambition of those kings, for whom Columbus promised the conditions to reconquer the Holy Land for the Church.

The imperialist enterprise of the Crusades remained in the past, but the mentality persisted. The logic of the movement survived into modern times and to this day it is still present in some forms of Christian expansion. The religious project, which extends mainly from the 11th to the 13th century, and only really ends in the 15th century, is explored by some historians as a movement that legitimized violence in the name of God, although there is no unanimity in indicating the religious motivation for justifying the bellicosity present in the enterprise.

The ambition for land and riches certainly was also a strong reason for mobilizing so many volunteers for the cause of the Crusades. It was, above all, a feeling of distrust in relation to the unknown, to what was different; in other words, a place that had other frames of reference, which ended up generating the insecurity that culminated in Western Europe organizing these expeditions East, to fight for and demarcate the frontiers of Christianity. Nayan Chanda writes that the apparent motivation was the "liberation of the Holy Land" from Arab rule, but it was also no secret that greed boosted the expeditions. The author comments that "perhaps the most shocking example of this covetousness had been the sacking of Constantinople by soldiers of the fourth crusade in 1204",[25] who stole so much gold and other precious things and provoked so much vandalism, that the damage and looting was almost impossible to count.

Spain, a great colonial imperial power, with Portugal, played a key role in the colonization movement and in the destruction of 'the other'. Todorov transcribes one of the last texts of Las Casas, famous for its imprecatory content, a mixture of curse and prophecy, as an illustration of feeling awakened and that until today has not been well resolved:

> I believe that because of these impious, criminal and ignominious works, perpetrated so unjustly, tyrannically and barbarously, God will pour out his fury and his wrath on Spain, because all Spain, good or bad, had its fair share of bloody riches, usurped at the cost of so much ruin and extermination.[26]

Despite this, Todorov and, similarly, Henry Dussel present Columbus as the man who inaugurates the modern era, leaving the mainland as an official envoy, in spite of all the contradiction and nonsense that surrounds his mission. It is paradoxical to note that, at the same time that Columbus is the first "modern" man, he still preserves the mentality that wants to give continuity to an outdated conversionist project and expansionist strategy that was being abandoned at the end of the Middle Ages.

In the course of his work, the author will include all of Europe and other settlers in this collective responsibility. Faced with so many atrocities committed, connivance or not, unfortunately we cannot but include the missionary practices of Christianity in this squadron of occupation and domination in the colonial period.

Las Casas himself was, at first, an *encomendero*,[27] a type of farmer with indigenous peoples in bondage [serfdom] when he arrived in the Caribbean around 1508. Subsequently, little by little, his worldview was transformed by contemplating abuses committed in the inhumane treatment of the indigenous people. In 1514, he had a conversion experience when he was confronted with the Holy Bible, when he was preparing a sermon for the feast of Pentecost, especially on the themes of "workers' rights", fair wages, and obligation to pay restitution amongst others. During this period, he renounced ownership of the indigenous people who were his possession and began a journey as a tireless apostle in the fight against all forms of slavery and oppression against the native people. This nonconformity brought much opposition and persecution by those who felt threatened by the possibility of losing the power and financial advantages of slave labour.

Few missionaries had the lucidity to perceive and prophetically denounce the barbarisms committed, amongst which the simplest were the transmission of diseases such as syphilis and tuberculosis. Few understood the difference between being Christian and being European, between Church and Hispanic or Lusitanian (Portuguese) civilization. They reinforced the messianism of the conquistadores, which mixed Christianity with Iberian civilization – which later made it difficult to understand the mission of the Church. An anti-mission perspective of these religious leaders is pointed out by Enrique Dussel, who contrasts their performance with that of Bartolomeu de Las Casas, who after his conversion had a differentiated posture of valuing and respecting the locals in work relations in the regions where he was installed.

Denouncing the cruelties committed by the conquistadores in the 16th century occupied most of the life of this human rights defender. His determination and non-conformism not only upset the settler *encomenderos* by hindering their interests, but also different segments of the Roman Church. His prophetic work is highlighted by Enrique Dussel, who comments that his texts are not limited to reporting the facts; they are an authentic critical interpretation of reality.

In 1550, the celebrated Junta de Valladolid took place, as an attempt to organize a document that could "define and justify the meaning and real reach of imperialist politics in the West Indies"[28] and addressed issues of rights and duties in bilateral relations between conquistadores and the colonized.

At that meeting, Las Casas was vigorously confronted by Juan Ginés de Sepúlveda, chaplain and chronicler of the emperor Carlos since 1535 and highly respected in court. This opponent defended the idea that "developed peoples" had the right of subjugating "savage peoples", ideas recorded in his thesis entitled "De Regno et de Regis Officio". This work served to strengthen and justify the "holy and just" wars in the West Indies.

In this controversy in Valladolid, it was clear that the two wanted the Christianization of the West Indies, but diverged with different interpretations about the means used. For Sepúlveda, it was necessary to "Hispanicize" the savages, and only by means of the Spanish mission, would it be possible to raise the level of life of the natives. The war against idolaters and infidels was considered to be just.

With a different approach, Bartolomeu de las Casas embarked in another direction, which started with the assumption that the human being is the work of the Creator, who made everyone free, and despite the peculiarities found, there is no inferior people or race. He questions, therefore, the assaults of the Spaniards in wanting to subjugate the indigenous people and subjecting them to servitude. Subsequently, the fearless work of Las Casas and his love for the indigenous cause were highly valued and cited by Simon Bolivar, who also came to be a symbol of liberation in Latin America.

In his work *The History of the Church in Brazil,* Hoornaert discusses this issue of hostility a lot and also the relative bellicosity prevailing in the evangelizing methods to convert the natives to the Christian faith, because the royal arms and the cross were intrinsically interconnected in this process. For this historian and theologian, "evangelizing" became the justification for the oppression and enslavement of natives, since "the warrior character of the evangelizer discourse also meant that the missionaries had no real interest in knowing and respecting the culture of 'others' to whom they were sent".[29] The evangelization was conceived only as indoctrination, as simple transmission of content without an interest in local culture, or a concern for dialogue, demonstration of love nor much less, an example of life.

The barbarism the conquered suffered was such that, not only did they face slaughter, theft of wives and lands, forced labour and more, but even when they fled, their executioners, who called themselves Christians. considered them subversives. Probably, many natives adhered to Christianity in fear of reprisals and punishments.

We can observe that, in the course of history, lamentably, the Church, in its missionary practice, has allowed itself to be contaminated and in some periods there was even a partnership with imperialist movements. At certain moments the Church forgot its prophetic role and became an accomplice of hegemonic projects that reinforced the denial of the identity of 'the other'.

Until the 16th century, the term "mission" was used to refer to the doctrine of the Trinity.[30] The Jesuits were the first to use the term to refer to the diffusion of the Christian faith between people, including Protestants, who were not members of the Catholic Church. In this new sense, it was committed and strongly related to the colonial expansion of the West.

David Bosch explores the mission by which the Western ecclesiastical system propagated itself to the rest of the World. The word "mission" was closely associated with colonial expansion movements; the right to have colonies brought with it the duty of Christianizing the colonized. This means that the colonial period was responsible for the great advance of missions, for it unleashed an unparalleled missionary age, which is also a sad inconsistency.

Now in the 21ˢᵗ century, we can see that the term holds a stigma, and in some areas even the word "Christian" has been interpreted in a pejorative sense, since it continues links to and is widely identified with imperialist expansionist movements, especially the misdeeds of the colonial period. Questioning the use of the word, just because it was part of the heritage of the history of mission, Hope Antone argues that

> the word mission needs to be removed from the Christian vocabulary. The reason for this is that the term "mission" not only carries with it great negative connotation (ranging from its complicity with colonialism until its aggressive stance in relation to that of another faith); it simply compromises the dialogue.[31]

In some sectors of the evangelical church, the possibility of an alternative nomenclature, expressing the same idea of Christian presence in the world to witness the gospel of Jesus Christ has been considered, since the term was quite impregnated with colonial logic. "Mission" presupposes three components: a) someone who *sends* (who is higher and has authority for this); b) someone who is *sent* on mission (invested with authority to do something for the recipients or even by the senders themselves); c) a third party who is the *object* of the mission.

However, the current crisis is not isolated in ecclesiastical history because, looking at different epochs lived by the Church of Christ, we realize that there have always been periods of cloudiness and turbulence, and we can also confirm that prophetic voices have been raised by those who had the courage to break paradigms by treading alternative and counter-hegemonic paths. We find examples of those who, by being faithful and consistent with their beliefs and their life project, were reneged on and marginalized, and not being in step with current thinking, suffered the attrition of incompatibility and antagonism. Many times they went through severe persecution, and some even paid for it with their own lives. They were the remnants of those who dared to think differently and to swim against the current of their time. They did not let themselves be carried along by the currents of dominant ideas. They are "inventors of new paths in the hegemonic power jungles", the nonconformists who "subverted the ways of doing things"[32] and did not comply with established standards. Whilst institutionalized power wants to implant uniformity and to fix limits, they initiated shortcuts which favoured plurality, multiculturality and creativity.

We have the classic example of the apostle Paul, who renounced his career and reputation in Jewish society to be one of the precursors of a new religious movement that emerged, deciding to live at the edge of dominant thinking.

Moving through history, we have numerous models of people who were solitary voices in their times, including one of the most controversial periods for Christianity, the Crusades; two heralds of love and freedom disagreed with the majority ideas proclaimed by the official church. One of them was Francis of Assisi, who gave up a noble standard of living to live in poverty and left a message to the world with his life. In the midst of that ideology of exclusion, hatred and violence, that led to a race to exterminate the Arabs, he also tried to register his protest. He undertook some trips to Muslim countries and managed to interact with some of their leaders. His trip to Egypt "was something more than the expression of personal interest or missionary zeal. It meant that a new spirit had arisen in the Christian world and that a remarkable transformation took place in the missionary methods of the Christian churches".[33]

The other who also lived at the time of the Crusades and walked against his time was Raymond Lulius. He was born in 1235, on the island of Majorca, and in days when his people nurtured hatred for Islam, he was one of the voices who did not keep silent, and argued that the annihilation of Muslims was a mistake and that the approach to evangelization needed to be revised. Amongst his "missionary proposals" – we might even consider these the first essays on inculturation and inter-culturation in missiology – he encouraged learning Arabic, which could contribute to an understanding of Muslim thought, because what really mattered was not simply the learning of a language, but to consider that this new knowledge could bring a new interpretation of that culture and also lead to an understanding of the thinking and doctrines of Muslims. He challenged the dominant missionary practice in those days and the methods used, signalling the need for a different mode of entering the Saracen world, which would be to give testimony of faith and life and not just preaching with words, even if it might cost one's life. Which is what happened to him: in one of his journeys to announce the gospel to the Arabs, he was so badly beaten up that he died from his wounds.

In different moments of humanity, it has always been possible to find those prophets who walked at the margins, concerned about the situation of their people, messengers of not only biblical content in order to fulfil an agenda of catechesis, but protagonists of an inculturated mission and true ambassadors of the kingdom of God, and who lived a style of life which taught through their attitudes. Sometimes they were heralds of protest that could range from "homeopathic doses for mourning to the 'overdose' of the greater proof of love of a Friar Montesinos".[34] We must not forget, then, that the question of imperialism and complicity of the mission is not restricted to a specific historical period. It would be reductionist to think that everything comes down to a problem in the relation of mission to colonialism. Nor can we "disregard the fact that this relationship is only part and parcel of the much broader and more complex project of the advance of Western technological civilization".[35] With the colonization movements, Western expansion was not only economic and religious, but also involved the expansion of hegemonic forms of knowledge that shaped the very conception of economy and religion.

These relationships were monologic – a one-way movement from the West to 'the others'. We now need to work towards empowering a "culture of cultures", argues Raul Fornet Betancourt. We lack two-way exchanges which make it possible to replace the hegemonic relationship with bilateral and multilateral relations, thus eliminating the traces of colonialism that characterized the contacts between North and South in the model of modernity, as Boaventura de Sousa Santos states, when writing that "colonialism is all exchanges, all interchanges in which a weaker part is robbed of their humanity".[36]

In this theme of otherness and monoculturalism, especially in Western missionary practice in contact with the autochthonous cultures of the "new world", Fornet Betancourt argues that there could not "be an intercultural or interreligious dialogue, since Western security to possess in its culture and religion the key of the absolute led to the spontaneous disqualification of culture and religion of 'the other'".[37] The unfolding of this position came to define the model of Western Christianity that, according to him, was absolutized and elevated to be the only possible expression of Christian faith.

However, common sense warns us that we will fall into error if we deny the importance of the role that Christian missions developed in the development of many societies around the world, including the great contribution of ethnographic and linguistic systematization in hundreds of peoples. Nevertheless, as we have already seen, we cannot escape of the weight of the sad heritage left behind and we have to admit the great historical debt of imperialist Christianization, which confused evangelization with the propagation of a lifestyle, with imposition of the values of the dominant Western culture, with the need to fulfil an agenda.

It is also undeniable that mission reached a level of complicity in this process of *coisificação* of 'the other' [objectivization – considering another person as a thing], which compromised the interpretation of the gospel message of Jesus Christ. The ecclesiastical leadership and a good part of the missionaries not only fell into line with contemporary thinking in the face of the circumstances, but also benefited directly or indirectly. Manuel de Nóbrega himself was against adapting to a simple lifestyle that did not contrast with the people in general and defended the possession of slaves for work in colleges and the use of force in evangelization. He "openly rejected the 'apostolic way' as a method of evangelization in the conquest of the Americas".[38]

In summarizing the colonial ideology, Paulo Suess writes that being colonized was a benefit. The conquered should be grateful because now under the leadership of the conquerors, even working exhaustingly and having their freedom restricted, they had "come to the knowledge of God" and received a guarantee of "deliverance from hell". The author even makes a severe criticism of one of Father Vieira's sermons, in which he states that all the suffering to which the native was subjected in the present was necessary for character improvement. The new life that they had achieved was a miracle, and for this great privilege they now enjoy "the conquered must pay the benefit of the conquest with religious zeal, with tithes and with works which include 'restrictions' on their freedom".[39]

Boaventura de Sousa Santos argues in his thesis that identification of 'the other' as a being devoid of knowledge and culture was the counterpoint of the colonial requirement to transport civilization to other peoples, that is, "the discovery of 'the other' in the colonial context always involved the production or reconfiguration of subalternity".[40] In fact, the great mark of colonialism and of current neo-colonialisms is the conception of 'the other' as an object. Colonialism leads to denial of diversity and is also responsible for the subordination and invisibility of the South.

We understand that the goals of the 16th and 21st century missionary movements are different. However, we find that the logic and motivation for the mission continue to be the same: I need 'the other' to fulfil my goals, because without it my goals are not reached. If, in the conquest, Christians depended on the "savages" to help to pan for gold – and these, in exchange, received the benefit of entering heaven – today churches need to work to increase percentages in statistics which reveal Christian expansion across the continents and their ability to save mankind. The real motivation is to exceed the hoped for [number of] adherents and not necessarily to manifest God's love, solidarity and care with the real physical, emotional and spiritual needs of the people who will receive the missionaries.

Missionary contact with the unknown, unlike the a culture of "visiting", was often characterized as vertical. Analysing various missionary movements in history, we have highlighted a classic example at the time of the conquest of America and that is one of the factors responsible for the shaping of the current mission model. The model of the evangelistic approach, as it was conceived, was a programme of catechesis and indoctrination, with transmission of contents, passing on concepts without respect for the human being who was being addressed.

Thus, the lack of concern with humankind in their totality may also be linked to a motivation which is anthropocentric and not Christocentric, that is, the discourse which only emphasizes the salvation of the soul reinforces the colonial ideology, since the events of this "temporal life" are not important and what counts is to attain the guarantee of heaven. In this model, there is an exaggerated emphasis on preaching (*kerygma*) and indoctrination and also an overvaluation of the spiritual dimension of life. Therefore, the non-recognition of 'the other' as subject favours the imposition of concepts and patterns of the hegemonic culture, since the other becomes simply an object of mission, there being no need for a dialogical practice of solidarity.

David Bosch makes a serious criticism of the strategy of the work still employed in our current time by the vast majority of missionaries and warns that mission must cease to be "a symbol of universality of Western imperialism among the new generations of the Third World, on the contrary, the present structure of modern mission is dead".[41] He also reminds us that the Church always needs to change in order to remain the same.

Commenting on the changes that are coming upon us at the high speed of broadband, Keith Eitel says that although the changes are there – and can and should be there – the future of Christian missions "will depend more on changes that are not made than on changes that are made".[42] According to Eitel, the necessary changes have not yet been made, at least in the macro movements, but need to be made, because their future depends on it. Meanwhile, we have witnessed in the "missionary universe" changes that are like make-up, papering over the cracks, which remind us of an expression used in Brazilian national politics: "Everything needs to change in order to continue the same".

There is a crisis of meaning today which has hit the Christian world like a well-aimed bullet. Evangelical communities, in their majority, have closed themselves in their ghettos and are talking to a world that already no longer exists. Few have a systemic view which contemplates humans in their entirety and understands their responsibility to contemporary society. The Church loses its reason for existence if it does not constantly remind itself of its need to care for its flock, but also its high priority and task: to be salt and light for the society around it, always remembering its prophetic role and carrying out its mission in service and dialogue.

This dichotomy is also brought out by Orlando Costas in developing the concepts of centripetal and centrifugal movement by the Church in the fulfilment of its mission, as

> a community gathered by the Holy Spirit to receive power and instruction, but also a team that is sent the world to learn how to serve it better, to give testimony of Christ with words and deeds, to be redemptively present in the struggles of the world and to call the peoples of the earth to enter into the kingdom of God.[43]

The mission of the church can only be understood in light of the kingdom of God, argues René Padilla. It is called to be an instrument of the kingdom through the continuation of Christ's mission to the world. The mission of the church is an extension of Jesus' mission. It is the manifestation of "the kingdom of God both through proclamation and through action and social service. Good works, therefore, are not a mere appendage of mission, but an integral part of the present manifestation of the kingdom".[44]

The thesis of Boaventura de Sousa Santos on the paradigmatic transition is a possibility for the reconstruction of social emancipation starting with the South and learning from the South. Perhaps it is here that the Third Church,[45] which emerges from the South, can play its part in the partnership for the construction of a more humane world. Boaventura argues in his work that it is not simply new knowledge we need, but a new mode of knowledge production. The emerging church of the South, which has the experience of having been colonized, may play a role in this moment of crisis and paradigmatic transition. It can reshape their strategies, review their paradigms and seek a dialogical model. It is possible to propose social missionary projects with sustainable actions – responsible ones that consider the communities not only in the present but with prospects for the future. It can also be a catalyst for the willingness to bring together inclusive partnerships in international networks.

Samuel Escobar, a Latin American missiologist, writes about a massive shift south of the centre of gravity of the Christian world. We are on the threshold of

> a new era of Christianity, whose main base will be located in the countries of the southern hemisphere, and where their dominant expressions will be filtered through the culture of these countries [...] now the Third Millennium will evidently remain under the leadership of the Third Church, the southern church.[46]

This missiologist defends a thesis on the existence of three different missiological schools or currents of approach, especially in the evangelical world. The first is *post-imperial missiology*, coming from the evangelicals of Great Britain and Europe. He called the second group *management missiology*, which has developed mainly around evangelical institutions in California, United States, which give strong emphasis on church planting movements, statistics and plans to "to reach all peoples"; being a typically North American school of thought, the quantitative approach predominates and pragmatic orientation is well defined. The third possibility is the *critical missiology of the periphery*, which comes from the old mission fields and now begins to impose itself on the questioning of the existing methods and models of mission. It is engaged and concerned with the agenda of the day in the world and "we could say that the basic thrust of this missiology is its critical nature. The issue for this missiology is not *how much* missionary action is required today but *what type* of missionary action is necessary".[47]

However, being a church in the contemporary world is simply a thorny and complex task, particularly for Christian mission, which is faced with problems and unusual situations of a magnitude never imagined, and which cry for answers. Perhaps this period of major changes may also be the most adequate one for Christian mission to move in directions which lead it back to the genuine goals of the New Testament. Facing strong opposition can become an opportunity for renewed contact with the original project of Jesus Christ.

The missionary project can still play a relevant role if it seeks past teachings and reassesses its continuity. In all honesty, we should review our approaches in missionary practice, recognizing our arrogance, which insists on thinking that we are superior and unique, and abandoning this "first day of Columbus" syndrome, which, as Bartolomeu Meliá[48] says, for centuries accompanies the ones who offer themselves to evangelize another culture with which they are not familiar.

The ideas of Bosch and other missiologists can contribute to the construction of new ways of being and doing. If we have ears to listen, we will take advantage of the insights of the first Christians who lived before the change brought by Christendom.[49] We cannot struggle anymore to preserve traditions without an honest reflection on the nature and purposes of mission, and especially on our need to reconsider our motivations.

2. The Foundations of the
Dominant Missionary Model

Analysing the Christian worldview over the course of the centuries, sadly we see that the church, in its missionary practice during certain periods of its journey, did not exercise its prophetic role, but was a partner in imperialist projects. It came to have a complicity with these hegemonic projects that encouraged the process of the *coisificação* [objectivization] of 'the other'. We also note that instead of this worldview, at different times, becoming incompatible with the models adopted by society, it has absorbed society's way of interpreting reality.

This chapter aims to show how some events, throughout history, and especially in the colonialist undertakings in the conquest of America in the 16th century, were determinants in imprinting a Eurocentric logic on the matrix of the missionary model of the Western Church. The objective here is not to report on the missionary movement historically, but to observe how some events in history can help us understand how this dominant model was foundational in the missionary practice that prevails today.

The contact between peoples and the consequent exchange of information which may result in changes in culture are facts that we can observe through the centuries. Nayan Chanda defends a thesis on globalization, pointing to the contribution of missionaries, merchants, soldiers and adventurers in these exchanges between cultures that this phenomenon, which for him are not recent. He shows how, over the course of history, these "agents of globalization" contributed to the creation of an exchange between cultures and also to the opening of bridges and interconnections between peoples and territories.

However, as we discussed in the previous chapter, some religious movements are also associated with violence, disrespect for the basic rights of human beings and cruelty.

Nevertheless, it would be unfair to deny the important contributions which missionary movements in the course of history have brought to humanity, including for the whole process of globalization of the planet, helping to make the world smaller, independently of positive or negative aspects.

Christianity and Christendom

When speaking of Christianity and the global missionary movement, opinions differ as to how to divide it into historical periods. As we presented in the previous chapter, David Bosch separated the epochs into a total of six paradigms, the last is still being configured, but it is already possible to identify some elements of it. Alan Kreider had difficulties in accepting this scheme and divided this history into three phases to refer to paradigm shifts in Christianity: pre-Christendom, Christendom and post-Christendom. One of his arguments is that Bosch's work also has three divisions: 1) the apocalyptic paradigm of primitive Christianity, which includes the early Christians; 2) the historic paradigms of mission: what the mission meant in successive periods over the centuries until the crisis of the western paradigm near the 1970s; 3) outlines of a contemporary mission paradigm that he calls ecumenical emergent.

According to Kreider, pre-Christendom begins with the first Christians and extends until Constantine in the 4th century. Christendom begins with the officialization of Christianity in this period and goes on until the beginning of the crisis of the sociocultural mode not only in missiology, but in the sciences in general. For him [Kreider] the third model, contemporary today, is still being drawn.

All of the text revolves around the reflection on the period of Christianity, since the author argues that the great change occurs in the second paradigm and, to the extent that the phases succeed one another, they undergo some alterations which do not compromise their inclusion in the same general model.

Although the purpose of this book is not to discuss divisions or sequences of paradigms in history, Kreider's thesis provides elements for this reflection that added to understanding the foundations of the missionary model especially in missionary practice and its approach to evangelization.

He considers eight categories to differentiate each missionary model and which also facilitate the contrast between pre-Christendom with Christendom. His classification is presented in the diagram below, which was translated and adapted to maintain the original idea in Portuguese.[1]

Strategic position – Christendom has changed the perspective of Christians from the margins of society to their centre. In pre-Christendom, before Constantine, Christianity was an irregular religion, not legitimized by the State. Christianity became the religion of the imperial establishment.

Attraction – The change of Christendom reinforced the appeal of Christianity with the imposition of incentives, thereby altering the nature of its attraction. In pre-Christendom, non-Christians were attracted by the freedom of the counterculture, justice and joy of Christians.

Power – The change of Christendom changed dependence of the church from divine to human power. In pre-Christendom, Christians are reminded how to trust in the power of God.

Approval – The change of Christendom transformed Christianity from a voluntary movement to a compulsory institution. The church grew from top to bottom. In pre-Christendom, believers came to faith and baptism, in spite of tremendous disincentives.

Inculturation – The change of Christendom led Christianity to "feel at home" in society, so that it lost its ability to make a relevant contribution to society, assimilating itself to it. In pre-Christendom, the word that Christians used to describe themselves was *paroikoi,* "resident aliens".

CATEGORY	PRE-CHRISTENDOM	CHRISTENDOM
Strategic Position	On the margins, in the opposite direction; services in private places	In the centre; accompanying society trends; services in public places
Attraction	Free people; attractive community; Spiritual power	Access to prestige; employment; participation in society
Power	Spiritual power; human vulnerability	Human power / institutional
Approval	Voluntary	Compulsory
Inculturation	Tension between autochthonous [indigenizing] and pilgrim principles; Christians feel that they are "foreign residents"	Predominance of local society's principles; conformed to the system – "feeling at home". Christian culture x local culture
Role of Jesus	The Good Shepherd, the one who cures; teacher for all Christians	Omnipotent- exalted with God; teacher for the minority of "perfect" Christians
Liturgy / worship	Simplicity in celebrations; Christians equipped to live attractive lives	Grand assemblies in imposing buildings to impress non-Christians; importance of rhetoric
Missionary style	Mission was the centre of the identity of the church; the search for dialogue with 'the other'	Mission is substituted by maintenance; Mission for deviated believers or for people on the frontiers

Kreider works with two concepts to explain the constant tension of the Christian life in society: an autochthonous or indigenizing principle – feeling at home in society; and a pilgrim principle – to remain faithful to the distinct convictions of Christianity.

Role of Jesus – The change of Christendom transformed Jesus' role as Good Shepherd and transferred it to the church. In pre-Christendom, Jesus was the teacher of all Christians; now in Christendom, he was the master of a minority of "perfect" Christians.

Liturgy / worship – The change of Christendom has transformed the worship of humble celebrations to grandiose assemblies, to impress non-Christians. The mark of the services used to be simplicity. The concern was not with great rhetoric, but in living the gospel.

The Style of Mission – The change of Christendom changed the focus of the church – from mission to maintenance – except on the fringes of "Christian territories". In pre-Christendom, mission was the centre of identity of the church and she sought ways to maintain a dialogue with its pagan and Jewish neighbours.

For Kreider, Christendom represents the institutionalization which consequently leads to hegemony. To be a majority allows a group to dominate and strengthen the sense of belonging, to enjoy benefits, incentives and win status. The church of Christendom is markedly different from the church which preceded Constantine, but its logic no longer finds space in the 21st century. There is a long way to go to fulfil the deconstruction of this format.

The British historian Philip Jenkins works on an approach totally antagonistic to Kreider. For him, Christendom is also related to hegemony, but he defends the possibility of a new Christendom from the Southern Hemisphere. Doing an analysis of this emerging Southern Christianity, he suggests that "the South represents a new tradition, of importance comparable to that of the East and West of historical times".[2]

This approach is reductionist because it positions Christendom as new ways of doing and being, and only changes the address of the dominant movement. At various times, with a unilateral vision from Europe, he makes it clear that he believes this new current of Christianity is going to be predominantly traditionalist and orthodox, but he does not reflect on the dangers of a new Christendom nor on how the church can adapt in order to continue being relevant in the contemporary world. He speaks about the South, but from the perspective of the North, without comprehending the type of growth that is seen in the emerging world.

Christianity, in the 4th century, thanks to the emperor Constantine, ceased to be a belief of minorities and became the religion of the Roman Empire. From being a persecuted church, she became the only legitimate religion. Christianity also became a political force, and the power of the State was put at the service of the missionary effort. The centre of gravity of the Christian religion became Byzantium, whose name changes to Constantinople in honour of the emperor. Rome began to play a minor role.

Constantine himself convened the first council of Nicaea, in 325 AD; from then on, the institution of dogmas[3] and the church "is now the church of the state, and heresy is a crime against the State. The consequence is that now, not a few times, not infrequently, the Church has gone from being a persecuted church to become the persecuting church".[4] Orthodoxy became the great mark of Christianity and it was no longer possible to believe anything other than that which was circumscribed by the councils. Whoever did not place themselves within it was labelled a heretic.

The empire was left with two capitals, and rivalry between Rome and Constantinople was not limited to the political plane, but also occurred within the ecclesiastical sphere, and the tensions grew until they culminated in the Great Schism of 1054. This is considered to be the "definitive rupture between the church of the East and of the West. It was sealed by the unfortunate Fourth Crusade (1204), with the conquest and plunder of Constantinople by the Latins and by the imposition of a 'Latin' emperor and patriarch".[5] After this, "the two wings of the church, one called 'Roman' and 'Catholic', the other 'Byzantine' and 'Orthodox', would follow different paths".[6]

Christianity was thus swallowed up by "Christendom", a new culture, with a new lifestyle more preoccupied with social position than with living ethically and in solidarity. Mission is centred on the church and becomes a vertical movement, a culture carrier, and no longer characterized by exemplary lives, which inspire and impact people in society by their behaviour.

It must also be considered that in the period which preceded this orthodox model the Church fought against Gnosticism, but there remained a remnant that reflected much of the fatalism of the time and influenced Christian thinking greatly. Material realities were devalued and the most important thing was eternal salvation. Bosch says that "this omnipresent ontological dualism manifested itself in pairs of infinite opposites: the temporal and the eternal, the physical and the spiritual, the earthly and the heavenly, the here and the beyond, the 'flesh down here' and the 'spirit up there' etc. Salvation could only mean liberation from the shackles of this hostile material world [...]".[7]

Augustine's theology, with his maxim that "the human soul is lost; so it needs to be saved"[8] has strongly reinforced this dualistic worldview which contaminated the understanding of salvation, and obviously the contagion also reached the model of mission, leaving its mark in the foundations of the dominant model that until today defines evangelizing pedagogy. Bosch specifies that in this conception the salvation of the soul, and no longer the reconciliation of the universe, is the centre. These Gnostic elements took root in our theologies and continue to determine not only missionary logic, but affect Christians in their daily living "because this reasoning is structured by an unbiblical dichotomy, generating the feeling of living in two worlds".[9]

From the 4th century onwards, monastic life, an initiative that had begun with the intention of simply living an integral life away from the course the church was taking, would now become a move that would also bring strong collaboration for the missionary movement, because it was a refuge for the preservation of many documents and a storehouse that produced a succession of people who were responsible for the maintenance of many ideals forgotten by the imperial church. It was in this way that the monks substituted the itinerant preachers and their missionary work contributed greatly in the conversion of different non-Christian peoples.

Monasticism was a fundamental agent of mission in the Middle Ages and not only contributed to the Christianizing of Europe, as Bosch highlights, but it also saved the medieval church from acquiescence and petrification. For the author, the monastic movement was the main instrument in the reform of European society "although monastic communities were not intentionally missionary (i.e. created for the purpose of mission), they were imbued with a missionary dimension".[10] Until the 12th century, the monastery was the centre of mission; however, the monastic movement was not well-regarded by some sectors of the church and, even today,

> missionary activity, because it is on the border of the church with other peoples and cultures, on certain occasions defies the structures of the churches that are accustomed to their cultural place – this is the reason why many of the church's stories, written "from the centre" pay little attention to the theme of the mission.[11]

The monks' lifestyle had a profound impact on the peasants' lives in particular. This aspect of "turning away" from secular and "material" life, was also absorbed and incorporated into the dominant model of mission, which requires that the missionary should live a life of seclusion from society, since their role is just to "preach" the gospel.

Simultaneous events take place from the 7th century with the death of Mohammed and the spread of Islam from the west coast of Arabia. Gradually, they conquered former Christian territories and reached the Iberian Peninsula in 711 AD, and settled there. In 732 AD, the Battle of Tours secured the advance of Muslims in Western Europe. The ideology of the Crusades begins to install itself on the continent.

In the 11th century, Europe was in an advanced state of ruralisation, with life consolidated in fiefdoms; however, without a strong central government, there was extreme disorder and much political fragmentation. The absence of an organized State became more obvious when the Arabs took the Mediterranean, preventing a more active commercial activity. The rural isolation of society reinforced the political power of local lords and increasingly weakened central powers. This was a strong mark of feudalism that propitiated the movement of the Crusades.

The Church, in turn, inheritor of classical culture, had the monopoly of knowledge. Its rigid hierarchical organization collaborated with the maintenance of power. Its estate was enlarged with the donation of land by the nobles and with the sale of indulgences,[12] which further increased its political power and made her a "great feudal lord". The power that the church accumulated allowed it to dictate standards of conduct, since it was necessary to maintain order and to ensure that the "divine will" would be fulfilled in society. In partnership with imperial power, they determined an intended harmony of social relations.

On November 27, 1095, Pope Urban II called the French nobles to a Council of the Church in Clermont, in an open space. The speech incited the gathered group against the Arabs, detailing actions taken in "holy places", especially in the holy city of Jerusalem. The knights were challenged to march eastwards on a trip to avenge the "sacrilege of the Arab savages" and rescue the city from their hands. Officially, there were no missionary intentions in relation to the Muslims, nor a desire to preach the gospel, but to resolve a situation of threat to the instituted power, both ecclesiastical and secular-imperial. Pope "Urban II, did not think of converting Muslims through military action; Islam was rather, a threat needed to be annihilated".[13] The mission was tempting because, in exchange, the nobles and their followers would receive the forgiveness of sins, the certainty of paradise, new lands, wealth and power. The church granted indulgences and other privileges to those who accepted being regimented for the mission of reoccupation or reconquest.

In addition to the Muslims, the Christian religion in the Middle Ages also fought against the heathens and the heretics, that is, those who did not follow the dogmas and practices established by the church. It encouraged some incursions giving them the character of holy war, as, for example, the case of the Albigenses in southern France, who disputed certain doctrines and practices defended by the Church. A Crusade was organized to stop them, and the "heretics" who survived the massacre had to submit to the Tribunal of the Holy Inquisition organized to judge and condemn the Albigenses.

As in colonialist expansion ventures with a civilizing mission, the effects of the Crusades left indelible marks in some societies, especially Muslim ones. In addition to massacres and devastation, the consequences are not just summed up as resentment, since European culture was enriched through contact with the East. This period created a great chasm between the world of Islam and Christianity and also gave a seal of approval to the mission model.

Eurocentric Project and Latin Christendom

From the 4th century, a medieval model was being structured upon church traditions. The simple and objective message of Jesus Christ was now fragmented within this universe of Christendom. Enrique Dussel supports a thesis about Christendom that sometimes intersects with the ideas of Bosch and Kreider. He argues for the existence of distinct geo-cultural phases in Christendom: *Byzantine Christendom* of the first centuries in the East, followed by *Latin Christendom*, which was identified from the 4th century and with the evangelization of the barbarians and Visigoths, coming to constitute what would shape Europe. With the invasion of Arabs in the Iberian Peninsula, in 711 AD,

Christian Spain reacts and in 718 starts a campaign of reconquest of territory in the name of threatened Christendom. This "holy war", through the reoccupation and advancement of frontiers, lasted for centuries until 1492, with the final conquest of Granada and the exit of the Arabs. That same year, Columbus "discovered" America and, encouraged by the conquests, the Spaniards only lay down their arms in the 17th century. For Dussel, although they are different times, they are part of a single process, for this people, who

> since 718 had been fighting against the Arabs, for seven centuries had been a "frontier people"; this is the same people who, in the year 1492, continues the campaign and advances through the Caribbean, afterwards the Aztec Empire, the Inca Empire and ends there, and only there, its crusade, the reconquest [...] Everything has been a single movement [...] In just one process, it is the same Latin and Hispanic Christendom that comes to America.[14]

The third Christendom is called by the author *colonial Christendom of the Indies*, different from the previous two, which were imperial and were at the centre of events, responsible for gradually organizing other countries at the periphery of the world. Implanted in the Americas, colonial Christendom, in its first phase of organization and expansion, runs from 1492 to 1808. From then on, with the emergence of independence movements, there begins a major crisis of colonial Christendom until 1962, a period when a new stage begins in search of identity and maturity, especially in Latin America, after interpretations and debates on the documents of the Vatican II Council (1962 to 1965).

Dussel sums up his thinking on Christendom stressing that "this great socio-political-religious-cultural movement is in the process of disappearing. This is the cause of all the problems and crises that Christians are experiencing in our days in Latin America",[15] although some still insist on maintaining the project.

The defenders of the European patent for modernity are accustomed to appeal to the cultural history of the ancient Greco-Roman world before the colonization of America, in order to legitimize its claim for exclusivity of that heritage. The curious thing about this argument is that it hides the fact that the truly advanced part of the Mediterranean world during that era was Islamic-Jewish. Furthermore, it was the Islamic-Jewish world which maintained the Greco-Roman inheritance, in addition to its cities, commerce, agricultural business, textile industries, philosophy and history, whilst the future "Western Europe" was being dominated by feudalism and was steeped in cultural obscurantism. Since 1453, with the taking of Constantinople by the Turks, it was surrounded by the Muslim world, which held much of the control of Mediterranean. With its very limited territories, it was isolated and in a condition considered peripheral in the world of Islam. This condition was determinant for Europeans to risk themselves in the search for other routes for trade. They became the "centre" controlling the new world that becomes its periphery.

The Latin American church was born within this general context of discoveries and colonization, already in a dependent situation in the midst of expansionist policies. Colonial Christendom was fully integrated into the capitalist mercantile system of the colonial power, increasingly accentuating the process of colonizer-colonized subordination.

We can deduce that Christendom happens when the "border" between church and State becomes very tenuous, and, as Hoornaert writes in describing the early Brazilian church during the beginning of the Portuguese colonization, "there was no ecclesial identification properly speaking. Vieira repeatedly affirms in his sermons that all the Portuguese are 'missionaries' and with this affirmation expresses exactly the self-understanding of their contemporaries".[16] Being Portuguese is synonymous with being a Christian, and the colonizer is the equivalent of an evangelizer.

Expansionism and Demotion: The Negation of 'the Other'

Commenting on the origin of the "myth of modernity", Dussel defends the thesis that the birth of modernity happens when Europe can confront its 'other' and so control it and beat it. The year 1492 "is the date of its birth, the origin of the 'experience' of the European ego to constitute other subjects and peoples as objects, instruments, which can be used and controlled for their own Europeanizing, civilizing, modernizing".[17] And it is precisely Spain, later looked down on by a good section of Europe, not actually considering it to be part of Europe, that champions the spread of modernity.

As we discussed in the previous chapter, Columbus died in 1506 with the certainty of having found the way to Asia via the West – a conviction that also persisted in other explorers and scholars. In European imagination, the contact established on the "new route" was with Asians and not Americans.

The event made it possible for Europe to define itself as a discovering "ego", colonizer of the otherness, demoting the conquered peoples and making other cultures their periphery. From that point on, Europe began to affirm itself as the "centre" of the world, marking the beginning of Modernity. This statement comes imbued with a feeling of superiority, sealed by the discoveries, because the centrality of Europe in the "world system" is not only the result of an accumulated internal superiority, "but also the effect of the simple fact of the discoveries, conquest, colonization and integration of Amerindia, which will give Europe a determinant comparative advantage over the Ottoman / Muslim world, India or China".[18]

In his book, *The Conquest of America: the question of the other*, Tzvetan Todorov gives an historical retrospective showing that the colonialist expansionist movements were instruments of destruction of 'the other'. For him, too, the beginning of the modern era is marked by the year 1492, when Columbus crosses the Atlantic and becomes the first missionary in that period. Sharing the same thesis as Dussel, Todorov interprets this "discovery" as meaning the "covering-up" of 'the other', the invasion of their territory, the plunder of their natural resources and mortification of autochthonous life. When commenting on the "discovery" of the new continent, he also makes a categorical statement that "the 16th century would see the greatest genocide perpetrated in the history of mankind".[19]

The founding of a mission model with a colonialist logic was a slow but effective historical process. In *The Writing of History*, Michel de Certeau portrays the chronological stages of the "modern" writing of history, and he is concerned not only with making a reconstitution of the chronological period, but also analysing the processes, including methodological deviations, which led to a distorted conception of 'the other' with fragmented discourses on historiography. He shows that short-sighted perception of 'the other' can lead to distortions in the relations of otherness and power. For this reason, concentrating his argument based on the etymology of the words (history + writing), the author articulates the relationship and the distance that the speech can maintain with what is real.

De Certeau takes as his starting point some stories of the historian Jean de Léry,[20] a member of the group sent by John Calvin to set up a special mission of colonization in Rio de Janeiro. De Certeau analyses the construction of the ethnological discourse by contrasting the "wild – primitive" way of speaking, constituted as 'the other', with the power of writing, a brand of society supposedly "developed", which can become a vehicle for expanding knowledge and confers superiority to the one who dominates this art. The impossibility of communicating otherwise than verbally confers the position of savages on this population recently "discovered", for "while the wild 'voice' is limited to the evanescent circle of its auditorium, writing *makes history*".[21]

The invention of the notion of savagery happens in the confirmation of otherness, the moment in which Jean de Léry thanks God for being above the savages in these newly discovered lands. This difference contrasts the hegemonic European culture – blessed by having received from God the special gift of writing – with the exotic savage world of America with its oral traditions. The standard which defines superiority puts the new continent on the margins of the "civilized West" as 'the other'.

Amongst many stories which display evidence of cultural shock, Léry writes about the efforts to evangelize the Native Americans in the hope of changing some "wrong" habits, and yet he fails in this pursuit.

These imperialist meetings are pictured by Tzvetan Todorov in his book *Nós e os outros – a reflexão francesa sobre a diversidade humana* [*We and the others – a French reflection on human diversity*], where he describes the monocultural vision of some thinkers in France, in questions such as: universal and local value, particular and general, unity and diversity. The author describes ethnocentrism as an "improper way of building universal values [around] the values belonging to the society to which they belonged";[22] they do so by deducing a universal starting with a particular. Whereas the universal should be the horizon of understanding between two or more particulars.

The conquered peoples were also made inferior by other factors, amongst them the idea of race, which Aníbal Quijano posits as a mental construct which expresses the basic experience of colonial domination. This author defends his theory that the concept of race, in its modern sense, does not have a known history before the colonization of America. It emerges as a new standard of power by the establishment of otherness which separates conquerors and conquered, superiors and inferiors, winners and losers in the idea of "race" – which is,

> supposedly a distinct biological structure to those in a situation of inferiority in relation to another. This idea was assumed by the conquerors as the main constitutive element, foundational of relations of domination that conquest required[23] and these "winners" soon called themselves "whites". The concept of race becomes a means of granting legitimacy to domination imposed by colonization.

Labelling the different as defective or inferior and excluding them from our world, is unfortunately a frequent human practice. We tend to "repudiate purely and simply the cultural, moral, religious, social and aesthetics more distant from those with which we identify ourselves".[24] Those customs which are very different from ours are considered atypical or abnormal.

The history of societies provides elements that can define a worldview characteristic of a particular region: each culture[25] interpreted, translated and organized into a system of values, beliefs, ideas, norms. According to Guimarães Rocha, these encounters with 'the other' can give rise to feelings of rejection, superiority, fear and hostility, and on the intellectual plane, serious difficulties in accepting the differences. Accepting the diversity of cultures and not overestimating ours to the detriment of others is the first step to avoiding the tendency to judge the culture[26] of 'the other' from the standpoint of the culture of the "I" or "my group". Therefore, we can accept the definition that ethnocentrism "is a vision of the world where our own group is taken as the centre of everything and all others are thought about and experienced through our values, our models, our definitions of what existence is".[27]

Lévi-Strauss states that, just as in antiquity segregationist ideas prevailed – those who did not participate in Greek culture were discriminated against and labelled "barbaric". Western civilization also used the term "savage" in the same sense. In ancient Greece, especially after the war against the Persians, the word came to be used to "divide the world's population into two equal parts: Greeks – therefore "we" – and the *barbarians* – 'the others', the foreigners".[28] In general, the barbarians were those who did not understand and did not speak Greek correctly.

In the same text, Todorov discusses the two possible meanings of "barbarian": the absolute meaning – the cruel foreigner; and the relative meaning – the foreigner who is different and incapable of understanding the language of 'the other'. By analysing some historical documents, the author tries to define who this barbarian is and points out several characteristics that could better describe the profile of this "kind of human being" and concludes affirming that "barbarians are those who, instead of recognizing others as human beings similar to themselves, end up considering others animals".[29] The concept of barbarity is therefore linked to the acts and attitudes of those who deny the full humanity of others, generally by considering them radically different from their own group.

Introducing the other side of the coin, Todorov continues by tracing a contrast between the terms "barbarism" and "civilization", characterizing the civilized, briefly, as the one who knows how to fully recognize the humanity of 'the others'. A civilized person is the one who knows how to recognize the plurality of groups, human societies and cultures. According to the author,

> another way of moving from barbarism to the civilization is to detach from oneself to be able to look outside [...] The withdrawal in itself is opposed to openness to others. It considers itself to be the only properly human group, refusing to get to know anything outside of their own existence or to offer something to others, remaining deliberately cloistered in its environment of origin, this is an indication of barbarism.[30]

Therefore, we must emphasize that barbarism is not restricted to some specific periods of history, much less can we use the term to refer to certain populations in some regions of the globe. According to Todorov, it is in us, and we all share the same instinct. It is a feature of the human being, and we are all subject to this estrangement from 'the other'. It seems to be something intrinsic to our humanity privileging our points of view and overvaluing our cosmovision. However, it is good to stress that it is the acts and attitudes which are barbarous or civilized, and not individuals or peoples.

Aníbal Quijano demonstrates in his work that America becomes the first identity of modernity and that this "novelty" has produced historically new social relations. Terms that previously indicated geographical origins or country of origin, such as *European, Spanish* and *Portuguese*, also acquired, in relation to the new identities, a racial connotation.

Considering that Columbus docked in the Caribbean inhabited by indigenous people and peasants, in what is recognized to have been the most primitive and poorest region at the time, this first impact of conquest would be decisive for the elaboration of his conception of 'the other'. Domination is soon perceived in the giving of names to places, without any concern that the people of the land had already named the place. The name adopted revealed the desire be in or part of Europe. Mexico, for example, was called New Spain; Colombia was given the name of New Granada.

Quijano severely criticizes the imagination of western Europeans, who considered themselves the culmination of a trajectory of civilization, the apex of development, the most advanced of the human species and creators and protagonists of modernity. As for the "remainder" of humanity, it belonged to a category of inferior nature. The great achievement of Europeans would not be just their feeling of being privileged, but it was their ability to disseminate and establish this historical perspective as hegemonic, within the new intersubjective universe of the world power standards.

In addition to ethnic cleansing and genocide, the greatest disgrace committed in these "cover-ups" and disagreements was the non-recognition of 'the other' as subject, since the great brand of colonialism and the current neo-colonialisms will always be the conception of 'the other' as object.

Boaventura de Sousa Santos makes an important contribution to this matter of unequal exchanges between cultures, showing that this has always led to the death of local knowledge belonging to the subordinate culture, a trampling of concepts that he calls *epistemicide*, the murder of local knowledge. It is "hegemonic globalization that cannibalizes the differences rather than allowing dialogue between them. They are trapped by silences, manipulations and exclusions".[31]

This sociologist, working on the dominant concept of mono-culturality, comments that for the construction of multicultural thinking/knowledge that operates in a new counter-hegemonic logic, it is necessary to consider two questions present in the encounter with 'the other': silence and difference. In other words, "how to conduct a multicultural dialogue when some cultures were reduced to silence and their ways of seeing and knowing the world have become unpronounceable?"[32]

The author defends an "ecology of knowledge", in which we cannot only share our understanding, but also learn other knowledge, thus combating all vestiges of dominant monoculturalism. We are compelled to seek non-conformist procedures that translate into counter-hegemonic globalization and allow local cultures to develop their own reference systems.

Colonization and Mission: Domination Which Silences

The implantation of churches in the colonial period among Catholics was facilitated by a treaty between church and state: the *Padroado Régio*. This agreement was drawn in the mid-15th century, from the Papal Bulls, which conferred to "Catholic kings the power to evangelize the 'infidels' in the discovered lands. From then on, the privileges have always been increased, including the collection of ecclesiastical tithes by the Spanish Crown".[33]

The kings of Portugal also had a guarantee in the right of patronage in the new Portuguese colonies. Authorized by the Pope to the Portuguese monarch, this "was to implement the faith in Brazilian lands. In fact, such privileges usually led to an identification between colonization and Christianization".[34] The result of this partnership attributed rights and special responsibilities to the State by the expansion of the faith into the territories it controlled, including influence in the appointment of ecclesiastical jobs and in changes to the limits and competence of dioceses.

Pablo Richard observes that the practices of the *Padroado* [ecclesiastical patronage] were beyond what is envisaged in documents, since colonial power committed abuses to the extent of controlling the inner life of the church as an institution. The church of Rome delegated the right to *Padroado* to the kings of Spain and Portugal, "since in the 16th century, it was absorbed, among other things, with the Protestant Reformation and by wars of religion. It is its weakness that forces it to delegate to civil power the Christianization of America".[35]

In the specific case of Portugal, the agreement between the Portuguese and the Vatican was sealed on January 8, 1455 by Pope Nicholas V, granting Portugal some special rights over their colonies.[36] The Portuguese and Spanish were looking for new routes to Asia, "and the Pope gave the Portuguese Prince Henry, the Navigator, the right to all lands south of the Tropic of Cancer for trade and conversion".[37] No missionary left Europe without the permission of the king, and they had to swear total allegiance to the monarch. As we commented in chapter one, colonialism and mission were interdependent. Rights and duties mingled, because colonizing and Christianizing walked together, as Bosch described, commenting that "this right to 'send' ecclesiastical agents to distant colonies was so decisive that the activities and designation of the envoys derived their names from this action: their assignments were called 'mission' [...] and they themselves 'Missionaries'".[38]

Catholicism was an instrument of political power for the monarchs, mainly from Spain and Portugal, because in addition to "performing various administrative functions in the state machine, the Church assumed an essential place in the sphere of education",[39] and was also involved with the large territorial properties that contributed to increase the corporate prestige in the most diverse spheres of social life.

The complicity of mission in the colonial project was a fact evidenced by several documents which prove it, including the financing of costly sea expeditions to "proclaim the faith". Hoornaert says that, using the excuse of the fight against Islam, the "great enemy", colonialist undertakings were funded by the "Order of Christ", "formed with the ancient funds of the very rich Order of the Templars".[40] The author comments that, still in the lull of ideals from the Crusades where they wanted to fight the enemies of faith, the same warrior spirit dominates the Portuguese colonization. This ideology of "holy war" meant that it never was really mission as such in Latin America: there was conquest, implantation of the structure of the dominant religion. Mission and conquest are irreconcilable".[41]

The missionaries were part of the expansion of the frontiers of the colonial system. They were transformed into true *"bandeirantes"*[41], defenders of borders [editor's note: literally, 'flag bearers', legendary pioneers of the expansion of

Brazil's frontier]. The order of Mercedarians,[42] for example, "only worked at the extreme north of Brazil, because of the express need to secure borders in the Amazon region, where the danger of commercial competition always existed".[43]

A group that did not align with the dominant order were the Hermits, a lay missionary movement that chose to stay out of the gold rush. Their choice of seclusion and poverty collaborated in their achieving strong respect amongst the populace. Because of this, they were persecuted by the colonial regime.

The colonial enterprise also established the number of missionaries who would enter the colonies, defined not by the real needs of religious orders for their ecclesiastical work, but in accordance with the needs of the colonial regime's expansion. The control of the growth of religious groups also happened through restricting the construction of new convents and authorizations in deserted places that could be of interest to the government for border security.

Missionary activity in the early stages of colonization in Spanish America was not under the responsibility of the Church, but, by force of circumstances, was left to the heads of the expeditions. The first missionaries to arrive were: Franciscans, Dominicans and Augustinians. The Jesuits were only able to enter after 1549, and were the ones that had the best results in overcoming the difficulties when adapting to the new continent, because they worked hard to learn the language and submitted themselves to living in the most precarious conditions with the people; they were "responsible for the most systematic and enduring missionary experiences in America"[44] and they were the only order that did not submit totally to the dominion of the Crown.

Of all the orders who have worked in Latin America, the Jesuits were the most independent in the colonial period and, for this, they also suffered reprisals. Their relationship with the ruling classes was very troubled, especially because, already in the 18th century, they had strong mobilization among indigenous populations, with the objective of resisting colonial exploitation. The result of this opposition between colonists and missionaries, with the connivance of some sectors of the Church was the expulsion of the Jesuit order from Latin America, in 1767, not only as the "result of some 'currents of thinking' born in Europe; it is rather the triumph of European colonial power over the organisations of national and popular interests, which already in the 18th century, gained shape and strength in Latin America".[45]

In view of the abuses committed under the *Padroado* regime, mainly by weakening the authority of Rome, Pope Gregory XV founded the Sacred Congregation for the Propagation of the Faith, in 1622, which became better known as *Propaganda Fide*. The goal was to centralize all decisions and strategies related to missionary activities in this congregation to be controlled by the pontiff.

One of the trademarks of the *Padroado* in Brazil was its contribution to creating a vertical image of mission. The new church was dependent on the monarch, who, in turn, was strongly influenced by a Constantinian mentality. Thus, impregnated in our culture, was the idea of a paternalistic God, because "the King, the local lord acted in the same way: as a parent who protects, solves problems, gives financial sustenance, shelter and finally controls everything".[46] This hegemonic concept also left a great mark of intolerance which characterizes our missionary approach in evangelization.

In this period, Catholicism became a compulsory religion, not only for the native peoples, because they had no alternative; after all, any sympathy for the Protestant movement could mean support for Dutch or English incursions. This culture of fear further invigorated Christendom, to the point that Nobrega himself was led to consider fear a necessity in the catechism of the native peoples and affirm: "Perhaps they will become converted more quickly by fear than they would be by love".[47]

The church was implanted in Latin America in a paternalistic context of oppression and dependence. This is an inheritance which presents us with no easy task in the sense of trying to circumvent this logic and finding ways to deconstruct a model that has been founded in these centuries of "coexistence between evangelization and colonization. We are far from perceiving the extent to which Christianity has compromised itself with dominating projects over the last four centuries".[48]

The discourse of the discoverers always contained a "missionary language". They claimed that God sent them to "save" the savages, or wanted to expand the dominions of the Church, or simply to dominate in order to reign. In the case of the Catholic Church, as a result of a troubled period of conquest, evangelization was also an imposition of new principles and became a justification for the oppression of those local populations who did not yet know Christianity. Historical documents further prove that "evangelization is almost always presented to us as an indoctrination and a cultural imposition".[49]

As a defence against the Protestant Reformation, the Catholic Church armed itself with protection mechanisms, and one of these was the strengthening of clericalism in the 16th century, an antagonistic vision to that of the reformers. This hierarchical concept, which gave little recognition of the priesthood of every Christian, would become a fundamental component in the configuration and strengthening of the dominant model of mission that prioritizes compliance with an agenda rather than relational evangelism. The concept of biblical vocation was also greatly diluted in this sort of clericalism, and today it has become an almost impossible goal to deconstruct this logic within the thinking of the vast majority of ordinary Christians. Tradition was impregnated with this perception and defends the position that being in mission is a task for those who are called, and in this case, only the pastor or the missionary are the legitimate agents of mission.

3. Formatting the Dominant Protestant Missionary Model

Chapter Two showed how some events in the course of history caused significant changes that, in turn, significantly contributed to the foundation of the dominant model of mission which can still be seen today. It is important for Protestant history to recognize that, until the Reformation in 1517, the Catholic Church was the guardian of the Christian faith.

This chapter resumes following the bifurcation [split; literally, 'fork in the road'] in the 16th century provoked by the reformers' movement, which gave rise to a new model with another matrix, but with the same monocultural and imperialist root that did not abandon the logic of conquests in the relationship with 'the other'.

Passing through North America, the Protestant model of mission, with the legacies and medieval understanding it received – now with the guise of the Enlightenment and greatly influenced by puritanism and pietism – is being configured by the socio-political changes that the country was experiencing. This model becomes the reference for the mission format in Latin America, especially in Brazil.

The Roots: Puritanism and Pietism

A brief study of the Reformation will lead us back onto the path that the Protestant missionary movement followed as it came to Latin America and, particularly, Brazil. According to Antonio Gouvêa Mendonça, it is essential to trace the "historical vicissitudes, which go back to the struggles of the Post-Reformation period, especially in England, as well as its repercussions on the formation of North American Protestantism, root of Brazilian Protestantism".[1]

Martin Luther, a German Augustinian monk, was responsible for the rupture with the Catholic Church. The fundamental factors that provoked this schism and came to influence the Protestant missionary model were: justification only by faith; individual responsibility of each Christian; priesthood of every Christian (because of the Anabaptists[2] Luther changed his mind later); and the centrality of the Scriptures in the life of every Christian.

After the Protestant Reformation in 1517, the Catholic Church was focused on the Counter-Reformation (Council of Trent, Inquisition, clericalization), while the reformers also concentrated all energy on the consolidation of the movement: probably the reason why mission was not a top priority on the Protestant agenda in the first three centuries – although some conservative scholars present an interpretation that does not spare the reformers from criticism for the "lack of missionary vision". Furthermore, it was deemed more important to conquer strategic spaces and demark territories on the old continent than to go out to evangelize the new lands recently discovered which were strongly marked by the Catholic presence.

Commenting on the desolation of the wars of religion to define which branch of the Christian faith would control a specific area, Stephen Neill points out that, until 1648, "the Protestants fought for the preservation of their own lives. Only the treaty of Westphalia that year ensured the survival of Protestantism [...]".[3] From now on, each region could choose its religion.

There were also many internal disputes within the Reform movement. Traditional systems of authority began to be questioned in Europe, and with the reformers "the dykes of ecclesiastical authority were broken, there was no way to prevent the flood of extremist positions ...".[4] Some groups radicalized and wanted more significant changes and were strongly suppressed by Luther's followers, as happened with the Peasants' Revolt in 1524, led by Thomas Müntzer. It seems that history did not teach enough for those who wanted change and reform. Experiences with the inquisition and abuses with indulgences were not enough to generate more tolerance in people.

At that time, the Anabaptists, dubbed by Bosch as the "stepchildren of the Reformation", were relentlessly persecuted. They not only broke the Westphalian rules but pursued the ideal of building a totally different church. The other reformers wanted to "change the Church" but not "replace it". However, "the project of the Anabaptists was not the reform of the existing church, but the restoration of the original proto-Christian community of true believers". Nevertheless, after a few years they began to be more concerned with maintenance than with mission. An exacerbated concern with correct doctrine, so present in the dominant reforming group, had already contaminated this group that travelled on the margins.

The fact that Luther argued that evangelization should only happen in areas governed by Lutheran leaders probably ended up creating a spirit of complacency with the idea of missionary expansion outside European borders. Years later, the interpretation of Calvinist theology, teaching that salvation was the exclusive work of God and that he predestined some elect for salvation, may also have helped to dampen down the flame of missionary ardour.

The Church of England, for political reasons, also broke with Rome and, from 1535, Henry VIII became the head of the Anglican Church. The ideas advocated by the Reformation in Germany, simmering in Europe and one of the strands of thinking in Geneva came to influence the British church. This was how a group who wanted a more profound reform in the life of the church, the Puritans, "achieved victories and came to shape the religious sentiment of the English people, and in this way [...] emigrated to America, where they would have a notable influence on the construction of a society to which they aspired".[6] Mendonça comments that Puritanism was more a way of life and a way of understanding the world "which has adjusted itself, not always passively, to the various currents of thought that would flow into the United States and prolonged by the history of Protestantism in that country and for their areas of missionary influence".[7] This ability to adjust to different socio-political conditions contributed to the expansion and deployment of new independent churches.

Meanwhile, Germany faced the development of pietism, which yearned for reform within the official church of Germany. The publication in 1675 of the book *Pia Desideria* [Pious Wishes] by Phillip J. Spener became a landmark and a symbol of the time, as it disseminated the ideas of Pietism, which was well known for its strong emphasis on personal conversion, holiness, social fraternity and the responsibility of witness. It is from there that the seeds of the Protestant missionary movement began to germinate.

Thanks to this movement, the idea of mission as a task of colonial governments was detached from the Protestant concept of mission. Now ordinary people were encouraged to total dedication and could participate in God's mission. "Pietism thus introduced the principle of 'voluntarism' in mission".[8]

The common thread guiding the missionary wave would come from the Danish Count Nicolaus Ludwig von Zinzendorf, who decided to shelter the brothers exiled from Moravia in his territories to avoid persecution. Years later, influenced by Pietist ideas, he would sensitize "his group" to the evangelization of peoples, and "21 August, 1732 is celebrated by the churches of Moravia as the beginning of their missionary work".[9] The Moravians were known for simplicity, spontaneity and pioneering spirit, travelling through inhospitable and distant places in the globe.

Meanwhile, an Anglican Church minister, John Wesley, was very enthusiastic and touched by the lifestyle of the Moravian brothers and also Pietist ideas. This notable experience in London, in 1738, represented a distinctive feature in Protestantism and also in the missionary movement.

The circulation of books in Europe narrating "the discoveries" and the exotic details of the trips helped awaken an adventurous spirit and a missionary consciousness, even if belatedly, in the Protestant world. The publication of *Mundus Novus*, of Amerigo Vespucci, in Latin, was well-publicized in Europe in 1504 and narrated news from America. At the time, Luther was 21 years old, and studied philosophy at the University of Erfurt.

One of the reasons postulated for the late awakening of the Protestant missionary movement in Europe is that the publication of William Carey's book, bringing a new perspective that would change the course of the Protestant missionary vision, came as late as 1792. In the same year, the Baptist Missionary

Society (BMS) was founded, who would send Carey to India the following year. Until that time, the idea that the commandment of Jesus regarding the "Go to all the world", also known as "the great commission" was accepted and accommodated as an order to be fulfilled only for the first apostles after the descent of the Holy Spirit, as narrated in the Book of Acts in the Bible. Carey is considered the father of modern Protestant missions, for being the first missionary sent overseas by a missionary organization. Carey himself was greatly influenced by reading English newspapers commenting on the journeys of the navigator James Cook.

One of his dreams was to hold a Missionary Conference in Cape Town in South Africa, known at the time as the Cape of Good Hope, bringing together leaders from different regions of the world in 1810, but his proposal became unfeasible, and was only fulfilled two hundred years later by the intervention of Lausanne III, held in Cape Town, in 2010.

Concluding this section, Pietism was largely responsible for the rapid spread of Protestant missionary movements in the 18th and 19th centuries, but perhaps in the euphoria of sharing their faith, coupled with the zeal for the maintenance of their principles, they did not manage to escape from the imperialist logic in their approach. The values of 'the other' were hardly considered and mission ended up becoming a cultural imposition. We perceive that on some occasions "the missions that arose from the Pietist movement tended to separate converts from the world and culture in which they lived [...]".[10] Such behaviour reinforced isolationism and evangelical dualism. Despite the undeniable value of the movement, this element would ally itself with other factors that in America gave rise to the dominant mission model in our day, which starts with the assumption of the superiority of the one who is on mission.

Implantation of Protestantism in North America

Spain and Portugal held the hegemony of the seas, making Roman Catholic religious imperialism possible, but they were losing this domination by the 17th century, when England and the Netherlands became maritime powers, which would favour Protestant expansion instead. The first attempts of the English to settle in America began at the end of the 16th century, but "the missionary purpose of converting the inhabitants in their new lands did not occupy a predominant role in their thinking",[11] although there are quite a few records of Protestant initiatives in preaching the gospel to natives and attempts to "anglicize" them. However, the logic is always the same employed in Catholic colonization, and "this conception would sometimes be so dominant that it became difficult to distinguish between mission and 'Westernization'".[12]

Protestant colonization would begin in 1620, but one of the first names associated with the evangelization of the Native Americans in North America was a Presbyterian named John Eliot, who at the age of 28 became a pastor in

1632, and, in the year 1646, "under the protection of Massachusetts Bay Company, began working among the Mohicans".[13]

Years later, of particular note was a missionary who would leave a very important legacy for the spread of the gospel in North America, named David Brainerd. He died very young, but the publication of his biography by Jonathan Edwards brought about a great impact and moved many people towards missionary work.

The Protestant emigrants who most influenced North American Protestantism were the Puritans when they left England partially in search of new possibilities, but mainly because of political-religious persecution at home. They wanted to build a Puritan society that would be a reference to other Christians. They intended to "transform this new land into a new Canaan, a place from which the kingdom of God could spread everywhere".[14] They felt themselves to be the people chosen by God, as Mendonça points out when he comments on the ambiguity of the group that left England in search of freedom, but now in the new world was exclusivist and intolerant of new ideas.

By this point, the Enlightenment worldview was firmly rooted in Europe. Life in society was no longer permeated by religion. The age of reason, with its beliefs in progress and emancipation of man, forced the Church to seek ways to live with this modernity. Humans no longer needed a strong God to help them. The controversy about the Church-State relationship increased. One of the responses of Christianity to the Enlightenment ideas, and that would profoundly penetrate the model of mission, "consisted in the privatization of religion. It would occupy a small space in public life".[15] In the private sphere, there would remain the subjective convictions, such as family values and religion, for example, and in the public world, only that which could be scientifically proven.

Pietism, with its emphasis on human feeling and experience with a hint of Puritanism in its tendency to isolate itself from the "things of the world", was a good way out of separating religion from reason. Over the years, the Church has resigned itself to this dualism. The search for a purer Christianity in Europe, through Puritanism and Pietism, soon spread to America, which had also been affected by this climate which stimulated what they called the "Great Awakening". The movement grew in density in 1734, marked by messages of repentance and holiness, especially by Jonathan Edwards. With the arrival of John Wesley and George Whitefield from England, their names became emblematic of that period. Over time, the ardour cooled, but by the first decade of the 19th century a new revival was already installed, called the "Second Great Awakening", which would have its apogee in 1858.

The theology that these movements produced, considering the changes the country was undergoing, would become an intrinsic component of North American Protestant thinking. However, the main fruit of these *revivalist* movements, according to Mendonça, was that they inspired new missionary initiatives and always produce a spirit of voluntarism, and in this case directly caused the missionary awakening of the 19th century. [16]

In those days, the mixture of perfectionist doctrines and the ideas of those which preached "separation from the world" further strengthened the re-appearance of dualist thinking and led to decontextualized interpretations of the role of the church in society. Emphasis was placed on the Doctrine of the Last Things and contempt for the present / earthly life. Mendonça says that in the conservative circles there was a certain fear, since the "discussions on slavery had gradually become dangerous to the tranquillity of the churches, and it is in this context that the theological tendency of not compromising the Church with the social question of slavery developed, separating the spiritual from the temporal".[17] Mainly in the south of the United States, there was a proliferation of discourses which softened the situation of slavery, declaring that these "subjects of political-social order" were not the competence of the church, which should only be preoccupied with salvation, conversion and other "spiritual" matters. The controversy over slavery[18] resulted in a division between the north and the south amongst Baptists and some other denominations. However, it is necessary to stress that not every southerner was a supporter of slavery.

The *revivals* had produced a relative unity among evangelicals, but the growing pressure of the Enlightenment ideas generated two antagonistic currents, one "emphasizing ecumenism and social renewal on the left, and confessional orthodoxy and evangelism, on the right. In the early 20th century, the first segment had evolved into the social gospel, and the second, into fundamentalism".[19]

Illogically, the defenders of doctrinal rigidity, preoccupied with inspiration and biblical inerrancy, did not question slavery, and the majority even defended it. The fundamentalists were so focused on observing formulas that they could not see the supremacy of love for their neighbour. Even to this day, they polarize the question of good and evil and are intolerant of people who do not think exactly like them. The movement strengthened in the first decades of the 20th century, with the publication of *The Fundamentals* brochures.[20]

As we have already seen, in encounters with other peoples, the western "discoverers" came to consider the differences as inferiority and, consequently, an open door to the enslavement of peoples. Even the Pope, in 1537, authorized the opening of a slave market in Lisbon, but the exclusivity of human trafficking was not only between Portugal and Spain. Other European countries followed the practice. It is estimated that the number of slaves "sold to the European colonies was between 20 and 40 million. And, in the meantime, the (supposed) superiority of westerners over other human beings took root with increasing firmness and was considered axiomatic".[21]

The Church was incapable of having a prophetic voice that condemned this inversion of values which transformed black people into a commodity. In the case of Brazil, from 1538, when the first groups from Africa arrived, until the promulgation of the *Lei Áurea* [the Golden Law, which abolished slavery] in 1888, the Catholic Church, which was already established and well-structured before the Protestants, did not do much. This resulted in diplomacy and accommodation for some, benefits for the few, and suffering for the majority involved – a situation similar to that of the church during Nazism, which, except in some cases, only passively watched the barbarism practiced by citizens and the governing classes.

In the United States, the question of slavery came to a head with the Civil War, from 1861 to 1865, which "was not properly a civil war, but the opposition of two civilizations and two conceptions of life, with the implacable triumph of one over the other, and with endless consequences for the future of the world".[22] The South, with six confederate states supporting slavery, lost the war, and a considerable number of these *confederates* emigrated to Brazil, founding a town they named Americana, in the Santa Bárbara region, São Paulo state.

North American Hegemony and Protestant Missionary Expansion

The predominance of Catholics in Latin America, as a result of their history before Protestantism, inhibited some initiatives to send European missionaries to the continent. In the 19th century, evangelical missionary organizations did not see this part of the world as a mission field, after so many years of Roman Catholic Christian presence. According to them, the strong Catholic heritage on the continent could hinder the success of Protestant evangelization. The Edinburgh Conference, in 1910, marks a milestone in the history of the missionary movement, because it was an attempt to organize a strategic plan for co-operation in global evangelism, but Latin America was scarcely visible because mission continued to be targeted on Africa and Asia.

It was only in the 1916 Congress of Panama that the "missiological abandonment" of Latin America by Protestants was recognized.

This context was conducive to facilitating the United States' efforts to keep Europe off the "continent". At this juncture, the Pan-American policy triggered by the American President James Monroe also known as the "Monroe Doctrine", with its maxim "America for Americans", was extending its influence throughout the whole of America. The subtle discourse that the United States had the "destiny" to lead and care for Latin America gradually crystallized, as we perceive, in the words of the senator G. Bacon: "We have an interest in owning Nicaragua. We have manifest need to take care of Central America [...] Let us know how to seize it, and if France and England want to intervene, forward with the Monroe doctrine".[23] Everything pinned on US interests and not on principles of solidarity, bilateral co-operation or consideration of needs of others.

The feeling of superiority over other Latin American nations was patent and is a subliminal message in the speeches of statesmen and other American leaders from that period. The sovereignty of these other countries was not ideologically recognized and the North American government apparently would be the ideal for all of America.

The Monroe ideology assumes great relevance, leading also to a religious interpretation. There is evidence "that the legacy of the Monroe Doctrine has strengthened, by the end of the 19th century and the beginning of the 20th century, the ideas of North Americans who thought of the articulation of the large scale evangelization of Latin America".[24] Up until that moment even the presence of the British Bible Society was seen as competition in territories of "North American domination".

With the end of the war between the United States and Spain, in 1898, because of disputes in Cuba, the North-Americans were strengthened as winners, and were now "convinced that the old vestiges of the Spanish empire should be replaced by the influence of Anglo-Saxon values".[25] Piedra cites reports of missionaries who were euphoric with the victory that put the United States at a world power level and defended "the principle which, in essence, led the United States to intervene and militarily invade Latin American countries, in other words, the principle of 'world police'".[26]

This concept was a halfway stage to legitimize the principle already incorporated in Europe of the "Manifest Destiny"[27] and a consequent neo-colonialism. The model Christian civilization (the United States) needed to work for the construction of "model states". The US intervention in Cuba was seen as a situation of liberating Cuba from Spanish rule and the missionary institutions saw a great opportunity to format the dominant Protestant missionary model of Protestant expansion. The same thing happened with the occupation of the Philippines and Puerto Rico, with the interpretation that there was a need for the implementation of a new religious system to oppose and clean up the Spanish remnants.

This ideology, which held to the belief in the superiority of Western culture, came to activate the latent racism in South Africa, contributing to the cultural devastation that would culminate in the segregationist politics of that country. Even the missionaries believed in the supremacy of the white race, believing the negros to be "the descendants of the accursed Cain, equality with them was out of the question".[28]

Even in the United States, in the post-civil war period, for fear of the large number of blacks who could rebel, evangelical leaders colluded with the organization of the Ku Klux Klan, and regrettably "did not lack preachers who would show their rejoicing. In fact, until a period quite far into the 20th century, most of the members of the Klan were also members of churches".[29] And it took quite a while to extirpate this racist sore that predominated most in the south, given the complacency of some pulpits.

The belief of Manifest Destiny in America was strengthened "by the North American acquisition of territories abroad and by its influence in the affairs of other countries and was one of the great supports of the work of missionary institutions".[30] History repeated itself, for the methods employed by crown of Spain and Portugal in partnership with the Catholic Church in the 16th century had plenty in common with the North American strategy and the Protestant church to justify the missionary expansion. They considered the new lands taken from the Native Americans and beforehand from Mexico, to be doors opened by God.

The United States believed that God, in his providence, had chosen them to have a strategic geopolitical role in the world and thus have new possibilities for preaching the gospel. The leaderships of Protestant missionary organizations also realized that the success of their projects depended partly on the socio-cultural influence of the United States. There was a close relationship between commercial expansionist strategies and the mission project.

The ideology of Manifest Destiny has its origin in the way that Calvinist ideas were incorporated into North American Protestantism, becoming something visceral that allows us to affirm that

> the construction of American nationality, in its spirit, is intimately linked to Calvinism considered in all its variants. Efficacy and success in action as signs of divine pleasure are the old norms of the Calvinist spirit and, surely, they were the ones that involved the ideal of the builders of a new scheme of social life in the North American soil.[31]

They believed that God entrusted the United States with the enterprise of saving mankind. Bosch comments that the Americans saw themselves as inaugurators of a new order which would last for centuries. The same commission given to the people of Israel was now transferred to the Americans. As in the late 18th century and early 19th century, millenarian beliefs were simmered in America, there was an urgency in the preaching of the gospel to all nations in order to shorten the coming of the kingdom of God. Christianizing society was preparation for the coming of this kingdom. It is in this context that Mendonça points out that "the ideal of the millennium would appear at the end of a process of social construction in which everyone in the whole world should participate under American inspiration and leadership". For this universal mission, which they received, to look after and direct the weaker people, it was "American Protestantism with its vast educational and religious enterprise, which prepared the way for its political and economic expansionism".[33]

Considering themselves a special people chosen by God brought along with it the responsibility to expand this civilizing project, so that the Puritan ideal of implanting the kingdom of God could become a reality. Saturated by Enlightenment thinking, Western superiors felt a responsibility to care for the "uncivilized". Both liberals and fundamentalists agreed with the strategy of civilizing as a prerequisite for evangelism and both "were committed to the culture of the West, which they propagated with equal vigor".[34]

This was the period in which there was great growth in Protestant missionary work, as a result of this nationalist sentiment and the influence of revivalist theology. It encouraged a spirit of sacrifice for the salvation of the world and conquest of regions for God, a theory that became known as "disinterested goodness", which, according to Mendonça, "seems to have really coloured the 'Manifest Destiny' impulse in foreign missionary areas, which demanded from the Americans the expenditure of large financial and human resources".[35]

Westernization was confused with conversion. There was an intrinsic relationship between being civilized and being Christian. The more like the missionary that someone was, the nearer to God and more "evolved" they would be. Mission was sharing the advantages of civilization and the American way of life. And this was also seen as the only way to shape the local people, to prepare the ground for the implementation of economic objectives on the continent. The completion of the Panama Canal, for example, has been interpreted not only as a narrowing of commercial relations, but also, spiritual union between the north and the south. It was like a memorial to "North American kindness" in consolidating this work that confirmed its "internationalism" and inaugurated a real pan-Americanism in the region.

With the entry of the United States into World War I, its position as a hero chosen by God was sealed, the benefactor who was engaging in conflict motivated by the purest intentions of defending and fighting for the weak. The idea of a "model nation" elected by God to "bless" the world was fulfilled. Unfortunately, the missionaries could not see the situation from another perspective, and this distorted view has greatly influenced the formatting of the Protestant mission in both its stance and approach.

David Bosch points out that in these encounters with 'the other', both liberals and fundamentalists shared the same vision of Manifest Destiny and, consequently, both fell into the same trap of treating people from different cultures as objects, not as brothers and sisters. According to this South African missiologist, there is, unequivocally, an organic link between the colonial expansion of the West and the notion of Manifest Destiny.

Protestant Missions in Latin America

The Catholic missions of the 16th century, as we read in Chapter Two, were sponsored expeditions organized by empires in partnership with the church, with the aim of subjugating and Christianizing. The Protestant missionary expansion of the 18th and 19th centuries was linked to companies with market interests, which had civilizing and evangelistic aims. Expanding became paramount for the distribution of populations, to seeking alternatives and renew the market – "an impulse which, without the introduction of the colonized in the circuit would run the risk of running out much faster".[36] Consciously or not, the missionaries in both periods have been used as useful fuel for the interests of the powers and as a vector for the imperialist expansion of the West. The catchphrase of the time became: "To colonize is to mission".

Writing about the history of evangelization in Brazil, Elben César makes a very simple distinction, but does not allow it to become a reductionist one. According to him, it is possible to divide history into three distinct periods: "In the 16th, 17th, and 18th centuries the Catholic missionaries *Christianized* the country; in the 19th century, the Protestant missionaries *evangelized* the country; and in the 20th century the Pentecostal missionaries *pentecostalized* the country (with the aid of charismatic Catholics)".[37] As this chapter does not concentrate on the shaping of the dominant Protestant missionary model in historiography, but proposes to study how the process formed the basis of the evangelical model of mission that prevails today, the placing is valid, as it shows that the information accumulated over the centuries became part of our frame of references. Although the approach has been quieter than in the first centuries, Protestant evangelization was also colonialist.

The publication of three works describing trips to Brazilian lands has influenced in some way the adventures of Protestants missionaries. One was *True Description of a Country of Savages* (1557) by Hans Staden, a German who was in Brazil twice (in 1548 and 1550). Another, that became an oft-quoted classic, was *Narrative of a Journey Made to the Land of Brazil*, written in French by Jean de Léry, when he was in Brazil with a group of Calvinists, and published in 1578, as discussed in Chapter Two. The third, many years later, which directly raised awareness and awakened missionary vocations in the peak period of Protestant growth, was *Reminiscências de Viagens e Permanências nas Províncias do Sul do Brasil* [*Memories of journeys and residence in the southern provinces of Brazil*] (1840), written by the North American Daniel Parish Kidder, a Methodist missionary who was part of the first attempt by the Methodists to settle in Brazil in 1837. They each are considered reference works because they contain details that provide a good overview of the colonial period and valuable information for Brazilian ethnography.

The books of those eras are always concerned with narrating their exotic experiences and describing "wild customs"; very little is reflected on the thoughts, feelings and opinions of this newly-found human being. With few exceptions, among them the texts of Las Casas, this reflection which does not label those who are different as "barbarian", belongs to an anthropology which appears in the 20th century.

Before the arrival of the first missionaries, Brazil received Protestants who were part of the pioneer immigrant groups, Germans and later Swiss, who when they established themselves already had a pastor with them. In 1855, the first missionary couple would arrive, Robert and Sarah Kalley, Scots of Presbyterian origin who would found the Congregational Church in Brazil. Then came the Presbyterians, the Methodists, and later, the Baptists. This presence asserted itself, not only aiding the development of the country with the establishment of schools and hospitals, but also producing greater religious diversity in Brazil, further restricting the dominance of the Catholic Church. In 1859, the first Presbyterian missionary, the North American Ashbel Green Simonton, landed in Rio de Janeiro, and in 1867, after several previous attempts, the Methodists are installed in Brazil. Although Mendonça states that the Methodist Church considers the date of 1876 as its official establishment in Brazil.[38]

Baptist immigrants began landing in late 1865, the year in which the Civil War ended,[39] but the larger groups came between 1867 and 1868. They were southerners from the Confederate States which, like other Protestant groups, were afraid of reprisals from the northern states and decided to emigrate to Brazil. They settled in the region of Americana, in São Paulo, and there organized the "First Baptist Church on Brazilian soil, in Santa Bárbara, on September 10, 1871, having the Rev. Richard Ratcliff as their founding pastor".[40] Initially, these refugees were not concerned with the evangelization of Brazilians, perhaps for the obvious reason of the language barrier. But the first two missionary couples sent by the Foreign Missions Board (today Board of American Missions), the Southern Baptist Convention United States, William and Ann Luther Bagby, and Zachariah and Kate Taylor, would arrive years later and chose Salvador to begin the Baptist work and to organize the first Brazilian Baptist Church there, in 1882, with former priest Antonio Teixeira José de Albuquerque.

With Catholicism well-established and solidly installed in Brazil, the Protestants who brought a "new religion" needed to unite to be able to survive in the presence of the dominant church, which had been in Latin America for three centuries already. Initially, there was co-operation between the different Protestant groups. Even in Europe, the first missionary organizations were interdenominational. Seemingly, crises unite people, as happened in the war in Angola. In the midst of the fighting there was no religious frontier, nor even interest in knowing who was Catholic or Evangelical [protestant] but we were united around a single project, in favour of life and survival. Domination and control lead to hegemony and bring feelings of accommodation, arrogance, competition and isolationism, amongst others.

The preferred strategy adopted by missionary work in Brazil was the organization of schools, as a way of reproducing the standards of American ideology. Mendonça makes some comparisons viewing the colleges as equivalent to the catechesis of the Jesuits, that is, instruments of colonizing action. In his text, he cites the arguments of the Baptist historian A. R. Crabtree, who advocated the importance of colleges to prove to Catholics the superiority of Protestant missionary education. "Crabtree expresses a conviction that probably was in the conscience of all the missionaries: they were carriers of a superior culture, which should be shared with other peoples, because it was the expression of the kingdom of God".[41]

In the missionary's imagination, Mendonça deduces, it was possible to reproduce the same successful recipe in Brazil: "If the American success could be attributed to the colonization by Protestants, Brazil could be placed on the same path by means of a cultural transplant in all its aspects".[42]

The misunderstandings between missionaries and nationals started in the early 20th century. There was not enough trust in local leadership to deliver all their responsibilities, because "the Western missionaries considered the peoples of the Third World inferior to themselves and, indeed, incapable to watch over the future of the Church".[43] Among Baptists, the clashes concerning autonomy in the management of funds, heritage, leadership positions and co-ordination in the Brazilian Baptist Convention took place in the 1920s, and were known as the "Radical Question". The regiments and statutes favoured missionary control over institutions, such as describes Pastor Reis Pereira, commenting that at these "meetings it is clear that most of the board members should be missionaries [...] Thus, the direction of institutions continued with the missionaries".[44]

Despite the questionable methodologies, in an attempt to reproduce strategies that Catholics had already used, it is impossible not to recognize the spirit of sacrifice so present in these first envoys in the 1900s – in addition to many deaths from illness, they submitted themselves to every type of deprivation.

It would be unfair to forget the achievements of so many of them, as memorials of the love of God in Brazilian society, as is the case of Pearl Ellis Byington, who, in the 1930s and 40s, worked hard for the disadvantaged and children, contributing to the founding of various philanthropic organizations, among them the Pro-Childhood Crusade, today the Pearl Byington Hospital, in São Paulo. Not everyone had dubious motivations or were silent in the face of injustice and atrocities committed. Bosch raises this discussion by leaving this thought: retrospective criticism is legitimate, but retrospective judgment does not fit.

The first missionaries in Brazil were products of the revival movements, therefore, their preaching followed these roots well, and was influenced by the style of preaching of those revival movements, which explains the strong conversionist mark to achieve the maximum number of adherents, although the

> pattern of preaching in Brazilian Protestantism was always threefold: revivalist, polemical and moralistic. The revivalist element was aimed at the conversion of the individual, the controversial element was to convince them of the truth of Protestantism over Catholicism, and the moralist element to show and inculcate the differentiating behaviour of the new religion.[46]

To this day, Brazilian Protestantism, specifically speaking of Baptists, has the United States as its reference and theological matrix [reference point]. And in this scheme, missiology was also covered. My emphasis on Baptists here is because this group has one of the largest missionary-sending agencies in the world: the American Missions Board, which belongs to the Southern Baptist Convention of the United States. After the whole journey of the missionary movement through history, passing through the Reformation, it was here that the current predominant model received its final form and comes to be the matrix of the paradigm mission in Brazil.

Puritanism settled down in the United States, having the dream of building a model nation, and pietism would emphasize the feeling of a chosen people that devalues the "temporal things". Subsequently, the revivals, faced with the need for a new attitude towards the current of Enlightenment ideas, would give the peculiar finishing touch that reinforces dualism in North American Protestant thinking. The contempt for "earthly things" and the radical valuation of "spiritual things" would lead the missionary model to a "practice with the primary objective of preaching only to achieve 'the salvation of the soul'. Dwight L. Moody created a motto that became famous and reveals how the church's vision in modernity was shaped: 'Why polish the brass in a ship that is sinking'? The world was like a ship sinking, with no future. The souls were the only things that mattered. So save as many souls as possible before the ship sinks".[47]

In this conception, the evangelistic approach that goes beyond leading 'the other' to manifest the desire for membership of Christianity is a waste of time, for we are saved for heaven! There is no need to create relationships or pursue holistic care, the body can suffer if the soul is already saved. This distorted and atrophied worldview has contributed to the perpetuation of fundamentalisms in the evangelical midst that concentrate their objectives to control and standardize their groups in obedience to creeds, dogmas and institutional maintenance. With this logic, what really matters is quantitative results. If the salvation of the soul is the whole of the justification for sharing the love of God, the greater the number of followers the better. Any relational emphasis or social responsibility can be a threat because there is a danger of "losing focus" of "spiritual things".

According to Samuel Escobar, this North American missiology has a quantifying intention, very concerned with statistics, schemes, goals, forecasts, all of which he calls Management Missiology. In it, the quantitative evaluation predominates and there is a well-defined pragmatic orientation. In order to achieve manageability, it is necessary "reduce reality to an intelligible figure and then to project missionary action as a response to a problem which has been described in a quantitative way".[48] It is conservative and with a strong emphasis on results which can be visualized in statistical diagrams. The methods and the fulfilment of tasks become more important than living with people and inspiring them.

The Crisis of the Model Today

As we have already described, according to David Bosch's thesis, the entire Western missionary movement of the last three centuries emerged from the matrix of the Enlightenment. Modernity, as the supremacy of reason, left its mark on the dominant model of missionary practice. Westerners believed they were more rational than other peoples and were therefore superior.

We find that it was this conception of superiority that fomented the ideology of Manifest Destiny, best embodied in the United States of America. Among evangelicals, as we have already seen, the Puritan worldview, pietism, and movements of spiritual awakening have added a pinch of exclusivism.

Another feature of the Enlightenment that would wreak havoc in the mission model was the belief in the victory of progress which was adapted and materialized in the doctrines on the millennium as the solution to the world's problems. According to Bosch, the belief that everything could be solved "is already at the origin of the emergence of missionary agencies based on volunteering at the end of the 18th century".[49] Western Christians held "the key" to solve the evils of mankind!

As previously mentioned at the beginning of this chapter, in the early years of the 20th century, two antagonistic forms of interpretation of the text of the Bible arose among Protestants who were trying to adapt to the constant pressures of Enlightenment ideas: the first group moved towards the social gospel, and the second towards fundamentalism.

Another factor which influenced the installation of fundamentalist thought, especially in the southern United States, was the end of the Civil War. The major academic centres were in the north, and generally new ideas came from those regions. The south closed in on an anti-intellectualism as a way of resisting the Yankee northerners.

Among the Baptists, this conservative group, very concerned with the "fundamentals" of Christianity, entrenched itself in the declarations and other codes and manuals for the defence of the faith, to "protect" its flock from theological liberalism. It is very probable that the dualist influence on the missionary model was ratified during this period. The fear of "liberal contamination" led the Baptists to a radicalism that came to shape the theology of mission, placing all the emphasis on the verbal proclamation of the gospel for the "salvation of souls", after all, life here on this planet has no meaning or importance. Our mission on earth is "to gather souls for heaven".

The conservative and isolationist tendency of some Baptists is a known fact. A segment of this church to this day does not accept being identified as Protestant, arguing they do not have their origins in the Wittenberg movement. We know that there are still radical remnants who see themselves as heirs of the first church in Jerusalem and of those who supposedly survived the Middle Ages by walking on the margins of the "Empire of Catholicism". This extremist line was also known as Landmarkism, considering themselves to be the only descendants of the time of Christ.

Throughout the 20th century new global challenges were emerging, changing the scene, and euphoria gradually gave way to a crisis. Traditional missionary agencies were no longer able to solve matters previously managed with ease. Their methods no longer worked. They needed to review their strategies. They were giving answers to a world that no longer existed.

To conclude, it was thought that the civilization model would solve the problems of humanity, but the world changed and fundamentalism was one of the responses of Protestantism to the currents it could no longer control. Fear of the new led some groups to close themselves away in their dogmas and confessions of faith, reducing contact with 'the other', instead resorting to the dumping of content for the salvation of the soul and implanting programmes; there is no dialogue or relationship of affection, since this presupposes equality to sit at the same table and decide what is best for everyone. The fixed idea for quantitative results conceals 'the other', reinforcing the suppression of their identity.

Today it is imperative to constantly review our real motivations for mission, thus avoiding the danger of falling into the trap of running after agendas and an obsession with statistics. If it is not for genuine love, 'the other' can become a fuel for the goals of organizations and missionaries. The West, which continues to reproduce colonialist logic, must pause to reflect and understand that the number of Christians in the developing countries is growing much more than in the northern hemisphere This emerging Christianity will require, to an increasing degree "the *status* of the dominant current, however much the Old World Order clings desperately to its hegemony in the control of information and public opinion".[50]

It is necessary to resist the temptation of quantitative evaluation which can divert the focus from the true motivation, which should be qualitative, because the essential thing is not how much we do, but how we do it. We need to be with people in a dialogical relationship and work *with* them and no longer *for* them.

4. Re-Discovering the Path to Dialogical Practice

Filled with Enlightenment ideas, Europeans believed that Europe represented the absolute end of history. The superiority of Western culture would prevail and all nations were headed for a single world culture. The "civilization" of the West has invaded cultures, swallowed knowledge; even using the missionaries to impose their customs.

This arrogance of "indolent reason" has been one of the subjects most debated by Boaventura de Sousa Santos, who characterizes it as "lazy, considering itself unique", exclusive and which does not exert sufficient effort see the knowledge and wealth of 'the other'. He makes some reflections, challenging us to work for a new logic and to escape from this Western rationality; that is, we do not need a new knowledge, but of a new way of producing knowledge. We need to revise our conception of 'the other' and recognize them as subject – leaving behind any traces of the colonialist logic; working for the construction of a multicultural knowledge that neutralizes contact with the hegemonic and monocultural silencer.

With the crisis of the great ideologies of the 20th century, among them Marxism, Capitalism and Fascism, fruits of Enlightenment Scientism, the dreams of the West have been frustrated more and more, especially during the 1960s and early 1970s. It was clear that the Enlightenment worldview was no longer capable of interpreting the world and that the hegemony of the Western thought was declining. David Bosch suggests a search for a "Post-Enlightenment self-critical Christian positioning" as the only means of neutralizing ideologies and giving mission some new directions away from the crisis in which it finds itself.

We have seen that, over the centuries, different factors colluded to determine the current configuration of the model of mission, but the North American participation in its historical journey was decisive for creating the brand of mission we know today.

In addition to reviewing the biblical ideal of approaches to sharing the faith, we should be alert to the warnings of the theorists of postcolonial studies who offer us other possibilities for a more reflexive action: how can one work within a new decolonized logic that opposes the continuity of a model that gives clear signs of exhaustion?

Escaping from Colonialist Logic

As we stated in Chapter One, modern missions originated within the context of Western colonialism from the 16th century. Agreeing with Bosch, the "colonial idea" has deep roots which began prior to the Christian era, "but this idea in its modernity is closely linked to the expansion of the Christian nations of the West".[1] The author argues that the missions became the support and defence of imperialism and the complicity is not limited to a specific historical period, but "is an integral part of the much broader project and complex of the advance of Western technological civilization".[2]

The partnership between the imperialist projects and mission was narrow, not even the Protestants escaped. It is sad to note that the advance of the Protestant missions is intrinsically linked to the expansionism of the Protestant powers.

Missionary practice in its approach continues to reproduce the Eurocentric colonialist logic of domination, which reinforces the denial of the identity of 'the other' and reduces it to an object. Despite some exceptions, the missiological model that predominates in these encounters with 'the other' has unilateral motivations, because what matters most are the objectives of the one who sends the missionary. There is no dialogical relationship in which all sides sit at the same table to talk and decide together what is best for everyone.

We find in the Iberian project, as presented in chapter two, a worldview that was settled over the centuries and took on a peculiar form with the movements of colonialist expansion in the 16th century. The project supported itself by imposing a "superior religion". The phenomenon of "discoveries", in turn, came to imprint in missionary practice a brand that would crystallize the idea of a superior race, since the discovery that 'other' people existed reinforced the advantage of the comparison. In the colonial context, the differences were interpreted as inferiority.

Another way opened with the Reformation, and this new face of the missionary movement accompanies the colonization of North America. The directions are different, but the logic remains the same – conquer and dominate. With the North American project, the model came to receive a format that became the matrix of the Brazilian Protestant missiological paradigm. Now, in the 19th century, what justified the project was also a superior capacity to know and transform the world. We inherited this feeling of superiority, which has been retouched there, in relation to non-Christians or to confessions different from ours.

According to this missiological model, in its meetings with 'the other', those different from us, the approach already starts with the assumption that the "visitors" are superior. While the Iberian project was predatory, the North American project was a "silencer". This silencing relation, fruit of the obsession of the "visitor" to "fulfil" its objectives, it silences and promotes the invisibility of 'the other'. This production of otherness in the colonial context consolidated the relations of inferiority and otherness. The feeling of superiority of the "foreigner" is so great that it suffocates and covers 'the other'. The motivation of the first was "to expand and dominate", and the second, "to reproduce a cultural model"; to evangelize was to share the benefits of Western civilization. One of the criteria for assessing the level of evangelization became the degree of adherence to the Anglo-Saxon culture.

The world of 'the other', very different from Western culture, was interpreted as demonic, so it should be eliminated, so as to start all over again by means of the Christianization and transplantation of European and American customs for the *savages*. The indigenous universe was negative, wrong, satanic – which became a justification, in the name of God, to destroy thousands of indigenous peoples in America. The culture was not considered nor the dignity and otherness of 'the other' respected. For domination and control, "the West's production as a form of hegemonic knowledge demanded the creation of an 'other', constituted as an intrinsically disqualified being".[3]

But we do not have to go as far as the 16th century to verify this type of situation. To this day we still experience strangeness in relation to cultural diversity. An example that shocked me greatly was at the time of the World Cup in South Africa, in 2010. A journalist from a Brazilian broadcaster, during a sporting programme, made a live commentary on the "irritating noise" of the horns [*vuvuzelas*] in the South African stadiums, stating that "it's good that the Olympics will happen in London, a more civilized place"!

This way of thinking was recalled by Dussel when he spoke about the method of a *tabula rasa*, which stated that local cultures encountered by the Europeans in the new continent had nothing to contribute to the process of evangelization and for this reason it needed to start from zero. This idea of European superiority above other world cultures is what the author calls the "myth" of Modernity, a theory widely defended by João Ginés de Sepúlveda, in the debate with Bartolomeu de Las Casas, in 1550. This champion of autochthonous rights preached the rupture between colonization and evangelization. He was the author of *De Unico Vocationis Modo* [Complete Works of Las Casas] in 1537, the first text to include the local culture as an active participant in evangelization, from being simply an object of indoctrination and charity. For Bartolomeu de Las Casas, one should seek to "modernize" the indigenous person without destroying their otherness.

Even if well-intentioned, the missionary may have a kind of practice which disregards 'the other's' world with its history, context, their knowledge and their experiences – the fruit of a colonialist conception, which Paulo Freire calls "banking". The missionary simply cares about dumping content as if downloading principles to 'the other', who receive this information and belief only passively. The missionary is the one who knows everything and disregards what the people of the place already know and do. It is possible to get some positive returns for their messages, but actually touching the heart of people would require a very different way.

Hoornaert references the project of evangelization as also being a pedagogical action. He presents two models used in missionary practice at the beginning of the colonization of Brazil. The "Holy Missions" was one of these and consisted of sporadic visits by missionaries to a particular community. He characterizes the other model, adopted by the Jesuits, as a "pedagogy of coexistence", because they chose to live with the indigenous community in villages. Considering that in intercultural contacts there is always the danger of imposing values of the intercultural dominant culture or decontextualized interpretations, the first strategy conditions the observation and does not allow a real involvement and friendship with the populations, the missionary will always be a visitor in that community. Already in the second method there is a greater interaction and acculturation occurs.[4] However, in this format, there is also the danger of the relationship being colonialist and of the dominant one not recognizing otherness and denying the identity of 'the other'. Living together may not be enough if the contact is predominantly vertical. A de-characterization of the dominated culture might even happen.

We believe that every culture has something to offer. It is possible to find ways to open dialogue between cultures, considering that everyone can participate as equals when they hear each other and recognize the otherness of each other.

However, the silencing relationship is present not only in the civilizing model and in the previous one, but also in the still-reigning conversionist model. The magazine *Theologies and Cultures*, a publication of Chang Jung Christian University, produced a series of articles that were the result of a conference organized to celebrate 100 years since the Edinburgh conference.

Analysing all of the lectures, we immediately identify ourselves with the contestations and the mismatches between the Asian theologians and Western missiology. Professor Choan-Seng Song questions the "world" of Edinburgh, which, besides having a western idealizing base, counted on 1,200 participants, 1,183 of whom came from Europe and North America. He recalls the speech of Bishop Azariah of India on that occasion, which was an appeal to Western missions to pay more attention to relationships and less emphasis on programmes. He also reiterates his words of gratitude for the sacrificial missions of the past, but states that the Western representatives at the event did not hear the clamour for rediscovering the path of dialogical practice of the Indian leader and "failed to notice the hope of friendship in the bishop's declaration".[5]

Likewise, as in our day, the people of India wanted to be loved by the missionaries. The people with whom we interact not only in our missionary endeavours, but in our daily life in general, wherever we may be, also want, above all, to feel our love.

Monoculturalism that silences is also a reality in North and South relations with people from outside Christianity, and not only in the evangelistic approach. The absence of dialogue is also visible in another more recent example in the Lausanne Movement. The organizing group of the third meeting held in South

Africa, in Cape Town, in 2010, were predominantly, leaders from the North. Names of Africans, Asians and Latinos were involved in the preparation and staging of the event, but the theological conceptualization, shaping of strategies and the definition of directions for the 198 countries represented, in total four thousand participants, was made exclusively by North Americans and Europeans.

In an evaluation of the Congress, René Padilla, in his article *The Future of the Lausanne Movement*, regrets that, while it is true, as expressed in the phrase which has become so popular, that "the centre of gravity of Christianity shifted from the North and the West to the South and the East", "the centre of organizational leadership, financial control and decision-making tends to stay in the North and the West".[6]

This was one more global event where it was very clear that the North still had the certainty that they, in the North, must decide in which direction and how the global church needs to walk. The United States, especially, continues to consider itself to be responsible for other countries and for the mission of leading nations in the evangelization of the world. Amongst the "apparitions" from the South that took place at Lausanne 3, it was Latin America that had the most paltry, sufferable participation.

The slogan euphorically proclaimed that this was "the largest world evangelical assembly" ever organized. While this is true, it does not mean that there was unanimity or even agreement amongst the majority. The work presented did not represent the opinions of many of the groups present, nor of others who were absent from the event. We were sitting there to hear theological expositions, conceptualizations and strategies that a minority had drawn up and defined as the best for all God's people on the planet.

The auditorium was composed of representatives of hundreds of missionary organizations around the world, including my own, the World Mission Board (JMM) of the Brazilian Baptist Convention, which enabled me to participate in the event. But I was able to confirm live that which I already knew through texts, that although the evangelical denominations have their peculiarities and different interpretations, in their mission model they act almost uniformly. The approaches are similar: authentic copies of the of southern conservative matrix in North America.

As already mentioned, for Boaventura de Sousa Santos, the hegemony is an attempt to build consensus based on the idea that what it produces is good for everyone. The author describes this persistence in exporting civilizational values to the South and says that "in the hegemonic perspective, this concept aims to force the rest of the world to conform to the economic, sociocultural and political rules imposed by the West".[7] This idea is closely intertwined with the idea of coloniality,[8] which always wants to decide what is best for 'the other'. The North still rationalizes within this logic of subalternity, in which the civilized superiors need to educate and feel responsible for the savages. Moreover, limiting and restricting opportunities for those who are emerging and peripheral to express themselves perpetuates the position of domination. It was this vision that helped to give leverage to the belief of Manifest Destiny, which, in turn, contributed to seal that sense of superiority and messianism in evangelicals.

Deciding what is good for others has to do with our real motivations. In colonial expansion, the motivation for achievements were profit, status or adventure. 'The other' was only rediscovering the path of dialogical practice, a means of achieving their goals. Today, we find missionaries who in their evangelistic contacts can deny the identity of 'the other' when they primarily look at people as an indicator for their statistics. They are unable to hear 'the other' and press forward focused on meeting their established goals.

In 2012, a Brazilian missionary friend of mine hosted some visitors from an African country at his home. The days were spent on medical consultations, preaching and conversations at home. Afterwards, the visitors confided in me that they wanted to visit some tourist sites in Rio de Janeiro, but when there were only two days left before their return to Africa, the family of the missionary decided that they wanted to introduce them to friends who lived in a place far from Rio.

"Showing" exotic visitors to friends was more important than asking them what they would like to do. Being able to present them symbolized a "trophy" for a person important enough to have visitors from another continent. The visitors had no choice but to follow the programme that the hosts chose. The Africans ended up leaving the "wonderful city" without fulfilling their simple dream of seeing some sights, but the will of the West was satisfied. This seemingly simple story hides a truth. The motivation for mission, many times, is ourselves: our reports, our personal projects, our image and others. I was very sad to find that this is the reality of many "mission fields" and not just one isolated event which occurred in a large urban centre.

To take away 'the other's' right to choose and decide what is best for them is what Boaventura de Sousa Santos defines as colonialism, that is, when "all trade, all exchanges, relationships, where a weaker party is expropriated of their humanity".[9] It reinforces the denial of their identity and the establishment of their invisibility. 'The other' becomes a fuel for the superior West to achieve their own goals and objectives.

Analysing the discourses presented in the reports of the travellers to the "New World" in the 16th century, Laplantine comments upon the different constructions ranging from revulsion to fascination with the exotic. That *ghostlike otherness*, according to him, does not have much relationship with reality, because

> the other – the [American] Indian, the Tahitian, more recently Basque or the Breton – is simply used as a support for an image whose place of reference is never America, Tahiti, the Basque Country or Brittany. These are pretext objects that can be mobilized both for the purpose of economic exploitation and for political militarism, to religious conversion or to aesthetic emotion. But, in all cases, the

other is not considered for itself. It is barely looked at. They [the observers] see themselves in them.[10]

In my 28-year missionary experience, I met excellent missionaries whose work is highly relevant and inspiring to all who live with them in those regions. However, I have to admit that Laplantine raises a controversial subject, which contains truth. Often, motivated by the obsession to follow programmes, certain missionaries do not think about the population with whom they are called to live. Practically, these people only represent statistics to these "envoys". They are "there on that side" living for the demands "from this side". I have also seen people use different excuses for travelling to far away places to see the curious and exotic. The "love for the people" and the "desire to preach" and to seek more conversions pass quickly when curiosity is satisfied, and the difficulties of cultural adaptation begin.

Increasingly, the North is being challenged to examine their motivations and, of course, this is a lesson for all of us. Some authors from the Southern countries are increasingly drawing attention to the message contained in the first letter of the Apostle Paul to the Corinthians which says:

> If I speak in the tongues of men and angels, but have not love, I am only a resounding gong or a clanging cymbal. If I have the gift of prophecy and can fathom all mysteries and all knowledge, and if I have faith that can remove mountains, but have not love, I am nothing. If I give all I possess to the poor and surrender my body to the flames, but have not love, I gain nothing.[12]

We are grateful to the missionaries who have often renounced their personal dreams, leaving their homelands to be an inspiration for our life projects, and many still are, but the sacrifice without genuine love for the people with whom we live may be useless. In this quoted text, the author points to a very simple path towards love that can lead us to an altruistic commitment of identification with 'the other'. The reason for the mission must be the glory of God and his love that can move our life in the direction of 'the other'. The love which led him to give himself for humanity, leaving his example for his followers: "As the Father has sent me, I send you".[13] Mistaken motives promote an anti-mission.

We need to bring the theme of coloniality to missiological reflections. The few existing discussion forums or publications always restrict themselves to talking about the role of the church or between models and forms of interpretation, but it is very rare to find proposals that show the importance of the recognition of otherness. It is appropriate to include on the agenda a discussion that values types of approaches and respect of the worldview of 'the other' who receives the gospel message. Even some texts or meetings of movements with a holistic understanding do not escape this tendency to spend the night hours studying theologies intensively, yet to not include in their debate the subjects of coloniality and the recognition of otherness.

These forums do not align with the dominant imperial model and do understand mission as a venture that will go far beyond the evangelical reductionist concept of "preaching to populate the sky", but even so, it is possible to identify some groups who have fallen into the same trap as the Western missionary model that predominates: contact with 'the other' starts from the preposition of the superiority of the envoy who is on a mission and moves from their own environment to help the poor or those who are different with solutions prepared by their own group. Consequently, the missionary decides what is best for the population. The following table is an attempt to contrast the two forms of thought with their variants: the missionary practice in colonialist thought and the missionary practice in decolonial thinking.[13]

Coloniality and Dialogicity in Missionary Practise

Colonialist Thought Fulfil Aims	Decolonialist Thought Dialogicity
Christendom	Biblical Christianity
Missiology as a part of Ecclesiology	Missiology based upon Missio Dei
Mission: civilizing *and converting* Reaching pagans Visits "their world" Educating the savages	*Dialogical Mission: relational* Working with women and men Living with them (interaction) Loving and cultivating relationships
Rigid orthodoxy Method: fulfilling programmes Looks for adhesions Vertical relationship	Local church Lives which have an impact through love Wins the right to be heard Dialogue and communion between equals
Ethnocentrism Epistemicide	Frontier culture Coexistence
Invasion of the "residence" Intolerance Marginalisation/ exclusion/ isolation	Respect in diversity Sensibility and Dialogue Include/ accept/shelter/share with
Projects to "help the poor" Working *for* them Decisions at the top	Partnerships in collective construction projects Doing it *with* them Deciding together what is best for everyone

Seeing the World from the Perspective of 'the Other'

Observing from the standpoint of 'the other', or thinking of the world from the perspective of 'the other', is undoubtedly the great difference for the approach of a decolonial mission as a Christian presence in the world. It is a relational practice that aims relentlessly to experience what Jesus said: "Love your neighbour as yourself" and also "so, in everything, do to others that which you want them to do to you; for this is the Law and the Prophets".[14] Thus, living with 'the other' is not only to make my projects viable, or legitimize my goals, but also a personal walk in a dialogical relationship built on equality, mutual respect and security in the love of God.

A hegemony, in addition to choosing what is good for others, takes decisions based on its goals for compliance with their programmes. The American International Mission Board (IMB), the biggest denominational missionary agency in the world and matrix of the Brazilian Protestant missiological model, especially of Baptists, redefined their strategies of action for the more than one hundred countries in which it operates and also changed the agenda of the missionaries without considering the opinion of national leaders and their mission partners, who have warned about the need to adapt the methodologies. This vertical decision, the result of a feeling of "superiority" that anaesthetizes and makes it impossible to listen to 'the other', imposes its formulas and sabotages the dialogue.

In the work of Paulo Freire, listening is a valuable virtue. For him, those who do not listen cannot talk with 'the other', restricting the relationship to a silencing monologue. Just by listening, we learn to talk to 'the other'. Listening means "permanent availability on the part of the subject who listens for the opening to the speech of 'the other', to the gesture of 'the other', to the differences of 'the other'.[15] For this, it is necessary to have a critical attitude and permanent reflection, including constant self-evaluation. Taking advantage of Freire's idea for the context of missionary activity, I have to admit that for some years I have also reproduced this hegemonic practice in Angola and today I see that many missionaries are still "doing communication" but not communicating with the people with whom they are working.

The priorities of the American International Mission Board are founded on three main pillars: oral preaching of the gospel, church planting and rapid training courses for leadership. Generally, the "packages" are considered ready when they leave the United States. They are strategies designed to achieve results in the short term; however, they breach various commitments which involved human and social development projects in the medium and long term because, in their final analysis, the soul is the privileged object of salvation and the body can be allowed to suffer. The real needs of these countries and what they would really like their American "partners" to do have become secondary because, in Western thought, these people are unable to make good choices on their own. The missionaries also recognize that good training could bring about benefits for local church leaders, but the time spent in this preparation can "disrupt the pre-established missionary programme". After all, we must meet the goals established by the matrix.

This logic is no longer sustainable and is quite washed out. Expansionism no longer imposes itself as before, but on the contrary, has only helped to intensify xenophobia in different regions of the planet. These hostilities have impeded the entrance of Christianity among some groups. Even non-governmental organizations also understand that to implement the programmes that they consider essential they need to listen to local opinions. And speaking of missionary enterprises, more rigor should exist in the implementation of intercultural partnerships, stimulating "respect for the experiential context and the sensitivity to demands and local knowledge as a starting point for any missionary project".[16]

These relations of power and domination, which we already explored in chapters two and three, structured to legitimize the conquests from the 16th century, have positioned 'the other', the non-European, as an inferior being. This was the establishment of otherness, and, today, to deconstruct this myth of modernity that everything that is not Western is inferior can take generations. For Anibal Quijano, these new social relations produced new negative racial-colonial identities in America, and one implication was that "the peoples were dispossessed of their own unique historical identities".[17] Mignolo, when commenting on these intercultural meetings says that the weakest party was always resigned; "They had no choice but to incorporate the European languages and European knowledge systems into their own systems".[18]

This "change" of identity occurred in different dimensions in Africa as well. Different kingdoms with separate languages and different cultural productions were randomly divided in the sharing of the continent at the Berlin Conference in 1885. Most striking was the situation of the slaves brought to America, who became simply "negroes" regardless of their origins. In each of these outrages, Christianity either watched from the "window" or participated in such practices. Fortunately, there were always some prophets who denounced and condemned such cultural vandalism.

During the colonial period in Angola, a specific example which illustrates what happened in many other instances was the denial of a group's identity to establish the dominant power through the regulations that accelerated the process of decreolization[19] and "made" the local population "more Portuguese". Only those who had sufficiently adopted the Portuguese culture were given Portuguese citizenship. The identity card certified that someone was "assimilated".[20] The other natives were not considered to be civilized, and to achieve basic rights in society, the majority of the population pursued this goal of being an "assimilated person". But the biggest theft of identity occurred through the obligation a person faced to exchange their family-given name for a Portuguese one imposed at the time of baptism. Imposing "a Portuguese name was not an exclusive characteristic of some Catholic missions. Notwithstanding the religious denomination, the interference of colonialism in the sphere of local names affected other Christian churches".[21] And in order not to enter into conflict with the missionary, the people submitted, but to this day they do not hide the bitterness this interference has caused in their lives.

Fortunately, today we have international protocols and documents which protect the diversity of cultural expressions and encourage interculturality, such as the UNESCO Convention, which has as one of its objectives "to encourage dialogue between cultures with the purpose of ensuring broader and more balanced cultural exchanges in the world in favour of intercultural respect and of a culture of peace".[22]

International institutions can play an important role as encouragers and as facilitators and moderators, to facilitate the birth of other forms of adaptation, new possibilities for collaboration between humankind, thus encouraging the awakening and recognition of diversity.

Writing on Human Rights, Nayan Chanda compares the human rights activist to the missionary, as both seek interdependence and work for the application of the idea that 'the other' is not inferior or enemy, but "'the other' is my ally, my relative, my friend. And what happens to 'the other' concerns me".[23] However, I would add that the task of the missionary is more complete and more arduous, as they have to constantly put themselves in the place of 'the other', the missionary must embody and show the example of Jesus all the time, everywhere and in everything they do. Their good example is because it mirrors the good example of Jesus. This is the great distinguishing feature of mission practice compared to non-governmental organization practice. This is how Jesus becomes the explanation for the missionary's motivation, confirming the famous quote of René Padilla, for whom mission is an action which requires explanation.

Transmitting concepts, transferring principles and creating extraordinary projects is a possible task for any missionary, but to inspire people using their own life as an illustration of what they say is a decision each individual needs to make for themselves. There is a popular saying in Portuguese "Words are convincing, but an example drags on behind". When the distance between discourse and daily practice increases, it reveals inconsistencies, and people have much more difficulty hearing the message proclaimed by the missionary. This is what Freire defines as speaking *for them* but not *with them*. It is as the biblical text warns, these people "claim to know God, but by their acts they deny him".[24] The example of life can be either a message that speaks to the heart of people or a denial of biblical truth.

I came to have a special admiration for the missiologist David Bosch when I got to know his biography more closely. I noticed that his work *Transforming Mission*, considered a classic in missiology, was not the result of academic research only, but the fruit of a militant activist journey begun in the 1970s, against the segregationist South African government's measures.

He studied in Switzerland and, when he returned to the country, working in Transkei, the same region as Nelson Mandela. His choice to be with the people from an early age put him in a critical opposition to apartheid, as he published articles that denounced racism and identified the system as a heresy.

He was a professor at the University of South Africa (Unisa) and collaborator with Bishop Desmond Tutu on the Reconciliation and Truth Commission of South Africa; however, he stayed in close proximity with the people and adopted a simplicity in his dress and a humble posture. He refused an invitation to teach at the Princeton Theological Seminary, instead remained in Africa and "preferred to maintain a 'prophetic solidarity' with the Dutch Reformed Church, even when he was effectively banned from their pulpits in the 1970s [...] he refused to back down to what might be for him an academic balcony". He decided not to be a simple observer "from the balcony", but his renunciations and identification with the people conferred on him the title of "street missiologist".

During the years I worked in the midst of the war in Angola, the periods of aerial bombing were the most exhausting because of the large number of people injured[27], because attending to them meant there was almost no time left to develop my "official missionary activity". But it was a time when I saw more people wanting to experience belonging to Jesus, and that was what gave us the sense of living and being in mission, despite all the devastating situations we were living through. The Baptist community played a leading role during the fighting, leaving "marks of its presence, especially in the fact they had stayed with the people in the city to be by their side in the most critical moments, and this was their most powerful message."[28] Several times we met soldiers or even civilians crying, and asking, "Why did you stay here?". When we had the opportunity to be withdrawn with the peacekeeping forces of the United Nations, we decided to stay with the people because "in war one is no longer owner of oneself, and still less when one has a commitment as nurse and missionary".[29] I often say to my students that the period in which I preached the gospel most, was the period which I preached less, in which I remained silent.

In a conversation with a missionary couple supported by our church,[30] they related the impact when a dentist visited the village where they live amongst the Macuxi, in Roraima, northern Brazil. They said that on her first visits the leadership of the tribe had made it very clear that speaking about religion was not permitted, but that they needed doctors, dentists and other professionals.

The missionaries accepted this and always helped in the village school and other voluntary services and did not speak to them about religion. They managed to take various health professionals, but this dentist became very popular in the tribe because of her respectful attitudes towards them.

On one occasion, she was attending to patients, and on seeing a precarious situation in the mouth of an indigenous patient, asked: "What do you want me to do? Do you want me to extract the tooth? Do you want me to treat the canal? It will need a dressing and afterwards you will need to go to town to complete the treatment. Or do you want to leave everything to be done in the town?". Afterwards, commenting on this dialogue with the missionary, the indigenous patient affirmed: "It is the first time that I was not treated like a horse. No-one has ever asked me what I wanted". He would be able to decide on his own how his treatment would be carried out.

Many civilized professionals normally only manage to see the patient's teeth, but not the person who is sitting in the chair before them. The missionaries obeyed the chief of the tribe and constantly visited the group to converse, act as professionals and participate in meetings at the school. Until the day on which they began to ask: "Could you not read 'your book' to us? Could you speak about your God?"

The couple told me all this with great joy. I perceived that they had fully involved themselves in the life of that village and now wanted to be with them, not only to share "some packages" with them, but were impregnated and constrained by the love of God, which impelled them and demonstrated in various ways what God had done through them. Before realizing it, they were working with the people in a relationship of respect and dignity.

The example that they showed through the way they lived their lives changed the religious rules of that group. Love prevailed, and they won the right to be heard, and, above all, created bonds. Their behaviour made a break with practices which silence 'the other' and established new possibilities with a dialogical, diaconal and relational practice.

Learning from History

The trajectory of the missionary movement in history was marked by inspiring experiences that offered expressive contributions not only in the personal lives of hundreds of people, but for society in every age. However, we observed how over the centuries disastrous interventions and practices have left stigmas and consequences that have compromised the reputation of Christianity to this day. And these events, in the course of history, contributed to the process of founding and structuring the predominant mission model currently operating in the world.

These days, we are living through a crisis in missiology, a paradigmatic transition, because although the present missionary model is no longer one of civilizing, the current dominant conversionist model is clearly out of step with new forms of communication. It is no longer able to impose itself, and yet also resists new ways of being and doing.

The resignation of Pope Benedict XVI in February 2013 shows that the future has arrived. The new Pope, Francis, already has signalled the need for a reformation of the Church in all its structures. Commenting on the election of the new pontiff, in an interview granted to *The Folha de São Paulo* [a major Brazilian newspaper], emeritus Archbishop Claudio Hummes of São Paulo admits that "the Church does not function anymore", and warns that the name chosen by the current Pope is meant to act as an encyclical. He admits that changes need to happen not only in the Curia Romana, or in liturgies, but in missionary work. He told the journalist: "This new evangelization needs new methods".[31]

History brings precious lessons to those who sincerely want to reflect. We need to learn from past failures, and one of the most important lessons that Brazil can extract from history is that, as a colonized victim, it should not repeat the same mistakes the colonizers made. It is now fashionable to say that the centre of gravity of Christianity has moved from the North and the West to the South and the East. While Christianity grows in geometric progression in China, the Philippines, and India are sending hundreds of missionaries, Brazil, mainly evangelical, considers itself to be the centre of the world missionary movement.

It is common to hear among people who "love mission" that Brazil is the next big thing and "this is the time for Brazil", "God is now raising Brazil", "the anointing for mission is on Brazil" and other similar expressions. They are maxims that can justify a newly emerging Manifest Destiny: Brazil as a new world leader, to save the world – the same pride which generated the North American arrogant messianism.

In missionary conferences and congresses, it is not uncommon to hear from some leaders, referring to the evangelization of the world in different periods of history, that the Iberian Project commanded the 16th century, and the 17th and 18th centuries counted on British leadership for missionary advancement, and then, in the 19th and 20th centuries, came the period of the United States, but now it is the "time of Brazil".

We need to revisit history with humility, caution and responsibility, also seeking wisdom from above to recognize our limitations and decide to listen to other cultures where we want to "do missions". We have to break this vicious colonial cycle and produce a missiology that reflects the learning experience of having been colonized ourselves.

But have we learned this lesson or will we reproduce the same colonialist logic and, above all, encourage the emergence of a new missionary empire in the South? Another question that comes to challenge us is: how can one break away from the Western model of modernity which stamped its matrix also on the mission and its practice? How can we manage to not repeat the errors which we condemn?

Modernity produced colonialist silencing contacts and today we face the challenge of risking new ways of evangelizing, trying to find innovative ways of discovering how the silence can speak, in such a way that autonomy is produced, rather than reproducing the silencing of the past. How to work *with* people and not any more *for* them.

Eliminating forms of vertical approaches, that subordinate and cut off the wrong attitudes that impose on others and make 'the other' invisible, is a decision that every Christian should make, without waiting for the definition of institutional models. We have already seen that the goals of Christendom always give priority to the preservation of structures and a theology of maintenance, not to engagement in the mission of God. Therefore, adopting a critical and reflective attitude and self-assessment can prevent us from reproducing the ideology of which we have been victims and allow us eradicate the perpetuation of these practices. It is always possible to work with people through co-existence in love, building together and subverting institutional rigidity, where necessary.

We can learn from the mono-culturality imposed on us to achieve solidarity and dialogicity. And to combat the model of monoculturalism, we ally ourselves with Boaventura de Sousa Santos once again, when he suggests the "Ecology of Knowledge" as an antidote, which guarantees equal opportunities to different sorts of knowledge. It begins with the possibility of diversity and counter-hegemonic globalization, and goes on to argue for more harmonious intercultural relations.

Outside the territories of historical Christianity, with new co-existence, we can learn other knowledge and thus make it possible to construct new strategies. Kreider makes a severe criticism of Western missionaries who have imported assumptions and institutions of Christendom as an integral part of the gospel in the deployment of these new churches in the South. Even today, in several African countries and even in Brazil, it is possible to find churches that require the use of suits and ties for their ministers when they are leading a celebration. I attended long African services, under high temperatures and outdoors, but the leader never presented himself without the full Western formal attire, because that was how "the missionary taught". The typical African costume was not considered spiritual and appropriate for officiating services.

These colonial churches had no autonomy in the past, and were totally dependent on western ecclesiastical authorities. They were labelled as being "second category" and to this day the task of escaping this heritage is not easy, since the great majority of Christians in these peripheral countries incorporated and assimilated this idea. However, at the same time that we encounter these remnants of colonialism that are incapable of valuing the wealth of local knowledge and of recognizing 'the other' as their equal. The leaders of the emerging world are increasingly discovering that they must listen again to their own cultures and realities and the pastoral realities they face.

Christian scholars are doing a lot of research on movements in the Middle Ages, but have very little interest in knowing about those emerging from the new churches in the peripheral world. The churches in the South continue to be invisible to many analysts in the North, but we must not forget that the majority of the Christian population will be living in Africa, Asia or Latin America, and their local practices will greatly influence the Christian churches in the whole world.

Another lesson to draw from history are the models of lived out missionary practices founded on respect, delivery and donation, as in the case of David Livingstone, a British missionary in African lands, who was the first anti-slavery European to travel into the interior of Africa. His reports about slave trafficking denounced the abuses committed, contributed towards inhibiting this practice and increased the conscience of the English.

Today, we have the privilege of having some non-governmental organizations who fight for human rights in defence of liberty and common ethical principles, such as Amnesty International, thanks to the strength of the pioneering vision of Peter Benenson in the 1960s, also in England.

Over the centuries, it has always been possible to observe alternative missionary models which have often walked on the margin of the hegemonic system, such as that of Bartolomeu de Las Casas, as already widely explored in this book. He was a pioneer in the fight for the human rights of indigenous peoples in America. He denounced the atrocities committed during the conquest and managed, at least temporarily, to convince the king to forbid forced conversion. Dussel refers to him as the first face-on critic of modernity.

Focusing on Brazil, we found at the beginning of colonization the testimony of Pedro Palácios, a Spanish hermit who accompanied the Jesuits in their first incursions. With his way of evangelizing through friendship, by co-existence, he did not fit the official standards of evangelization among the natives. Other hermits also received a lot of popular respect because of their simple lifestyle separated from wealth and power, but this isolation also led to many being persecuted by the colonial regime.

What about the persecution faced by the Jesuits in the 18th century, culminating in the expulsion of hundreds of them from Brazil and the subsequent arrest of dozens of priests? Some were killed, such as Gabriel Malagrida, burned in 1761 because he dared to contest the Marquis de Pombal; and the Capuchin Martinho de Nantes, considered subversive for protecting indigenous people against the strategies of the Bandeirantes, notwithstanding his own attitudes being also colonialist, considering the natives to be "more animals than men".

Antonio Vieira himself, who is often quoted and who achieved the title proclaimer of the justice of God, had his life marked by ambiguities. Indigenous people simply did not exist for him outside the Portuguese colonial project. They are a presence which nothing can alter or add to, for this celebrated monk, confirming one of the theories of Hoornaert, who claimed that the great sin of modern Europe is to "start with its own place, its own home, from the organization of its own household, and to establish this organization in a totalizing universal principle. This mentality, the one that Vieira had, is the colonial mentality which has always existed."[32] They simply "invaded the house of 'the other'" imposing their customs and rules.

Entering this path of non-recognition of otherness, another famous person who had a distorted view about 'the other' was Father Manoel da Nobrega, who stated that the native was only good when he had very little of their characteristics. The more like the Portuguese, the better they would be. In his logic, anything different is wrong. Anchieta also followed the same line, since his letters also reveal this evaluation of the native only being good when they were similar to the settlers.

For Hoornaert, the analysis of these discourses reveals the reductionist approach that permeates the understanding of missionary practice within the colonial system: reducing 'the other' to 'the same' through speeches, rites and symbols. This author's research also shows that in these writings there is a dichotomous relationship between colonizer and colonized, conversion and treasonous agreement. For the settlers, the traitor is the one who does not join the colonial project, who does not recognize the rules unilaterally made by the Portuguese and who does not accept Christianity. For some indigenous people, the traitor is the local person who "passes over to the other side", assimilating Portuguese culture and converting to Christianity.

History brings warnings and we can learn from previous mistakes if we start with a reflective and humble attitude, with a call to repentance and the willingness to fight against individualism inspired by the Enlightenment, and arrogance inherited from the imperialist expansionist movements, to follow the path to interdependence in relations. David Bosch argues that to break with these fetters, it is necessary that

> we reaffirm the indispensability of the conviction and the commitment [...] we need to recover the proximity, the interdependence, the symbiosis. The individual is not a monad, but part of a body [...] Only together will we save ourselves and we will survive. This involves not only a new relationship with nature, but also among human beings.[33]

The mission from the South can use the great biblical and historical models of Jesus, the incarnated Christ who emptied himself to reach man, or Paul, who did everything and was everything to be a witness of grace, or even St. Francis, or Mother Teresa of Calcutta, or the many other witnesses that history presents to us.

Acting in autochthonous partnerships, non-hegemonic networks, attuned to the signs of the times, it will be possible to work with the local people and not simply for them.

Looking for Biblical Models

The purpose of this book is not only to point out inconsistencies, breaches or simply indicate a new model, but to find alternatives that recover the ideal of God's original design by valuing good initiatives in history and rejecting experiences that have tarnished missionary practice. I have no intention to propose an ideal biblical model, but to invite the reader on an investigative journey which attempts to retrieve the relevance of the mission project from the Bible.

Beginning with the term "mission", we need to rethink its use. For fifteen hundred years, the church did not use this word with its current meaning. "Mission" has its origin in the context of colonialism. The word, as it is used today to refer to the proclamation of the gospel among people who do not know Jesus Christ, began to be employed in the 16th century by the Jesuits to designate the activities of the "ecclesiastical envoys" to offshore colonies. Ignatius of Loyola was the first to use the term to designate this task, because during the first fifteen centuries of Christianity were used different terminologies to refer to what we now call "mission": expressions like "propagation of the faith" have been used, and "preaching the gospel", "apostolic proclamation", amongst others.

The Royal Patronage agreement between state and church established that the right to have colonies overlapped with the duty to Christianize the "colonized savage". European agents were sent to the colonies with this "mission", and precisely from this attribution derived the name of the action. Therefore, the word has a direct relation with the colonial expansion of the West.

The term "mission" (in Latin, *missio*), until the period of the colonialist expansionist movements in the 16th century, was employed "exclusively with reference to the doctrine of the Trinity, that is, to the sending of the Son by the Father and the Holy Spirit by the Father and the Son."[34] This classic doctrine of *Missio Dei* has gone through a profound examination in the last century, especially after Karl Barth presented a paper in Brandenburg in 1932, defining mission as the action of God in the world. Subsequently, in 1952, at the Willingen Conference, the idea of *Missio Dei* was better articulated in the context of the doctrine of the Trinity. The concept was amplified as the Trinity sending the church into the world.

Thinking about mission starting with *Missio Dei* and not conforming to the simplistic classification within ecclesiology gives us a more holistic view and brings more relational and less managerial approaches. The protagonist of mission is no longer the missionary agency, or the local church or the missionary, but God himself. Being in mission is no longer only the actions of the church for the "non-Christians", but a commitment and a total partnership with what God wants to do in the world. In line with Bosch's thinking, it is an involvement in the movement of God's love for humanity.

Here we need to differentiate between mission and missions. There is a difference between "doing missions" and being on "mission". The use in the plural refers to the efforts of the Church to carry out the mission of God, to participate in the *Missio Dei*. The Church is a participant in God's intentions and purposes for the world, and therefore their goals must go beyond the ultimate goal of planting churches and the salvation of souls. This is a part of mission. The conversionist model, because of its dualistic worldview, despises everything that belongs to the "physical world" and prioritizes only speech that can lead the "souls to heaven". It is necessary to be very careful with this missionary dogma, because it reproduces the rhetoric of modernity, which, in order to subjugate peoples, promised salvation for all and reinforced dualism which gradually limited the action of the church to a long way from public life.

As we saw in chapter three, this managerial missiology, the matrix of the dominant model, has a reductionist conception that limits mission to proclamation and church growth. This model has a motivation to fulfil programmes, and 'the other' can become just a fuel for reaching the goals of organizations. The obsession for results masks 'the other'. It is enough for them to repeat some concepts, which automatically enters them into our statistics, whilst their socio-emotional, and very often even their spiritual dimension, are of little interest. This approach sectorizes and separates fragments from the whole. Bosch warns us to flee from this ecclesio-centric logic, to broaden our eyes and to seek a systemic vision, for "the mission is to turn from God to the world in regard to creation, conservation, redemption and consummation".[35]

Participating in God's mission or being in the mission of God is to read and interpret the biblical text as a unit, a story that has a sequence, and not to support a theology of mission fragmented from some verses of the Bible, with the argument of obedience to evangelize. The dominant model gives a disproportionate emphasis to a single Bible verse, which is the so-called "Great Commission": "Go therefore and make disciples of all nations, baptizing them in the name of the Father and the Son and the Holy Spirit, teaching them to obey all that I commanded you. And surely I am with you always, to the very end of the age."[36] Moreover, interpretation has prioritized only part of the teaching of this message. Jesus ordered us to teach *all* the things which he had commanded, but the great majority of church members believe in fulfilling a fragment of the text, sending people to "preach", is understood as "the whole" of the mission of the church.

The Church, in some way, is also a continuation of the mission of the prophets and of Jesus himself. From this perspective, we can observe the responsibility and the full task by understanding that mission is not only for non-believers but covers the whole of creation. The church is called to participate actively with all humanity in the mission of caring for creation, to recognize itself as a part of the creator's work, but also responsible for the common house that we inhabit.

Conservative groups lean more towards the *kerygmatic* model, which prioritizes almost exclusively oral preaching for evangelization. They interpret the message contained in the Great Commission as an order to "catch souls" with the use of some words which, most of the time, follow a formula. Leadership representatives of different contemporary tendencies polemicize about the dichotomy between evangelization and social action. Some insist that the priority is the verbal announcement of the gospel, whereas both actions should be inseparable. This is because both what is announced in words and that which is involved in service to the neighbor, are engaged in mission. The Holy Spirit uses each one as he pleases.

In the following chart, the missiologist David Hesselgrave poses three possibilities for missiological responses to the poor, but does not acknowledge that our relationships, attitudes, postures and actions in general are also part of evangelization.

Analyzing this diagram, we realize that Hesselgrave cannot escape from the logic of conversion, in which to obey a programme is more important than to demonstrate the love of God in different ways. Speaking and making are worth more than being. The extremist positions presented by him are evident, because Liberation Theology indeed "campaigned for pastoral activity which is nourished by a critical theological reflection and is social and societal in scope beyond the private sphere,"[37] but, in my opinion, did not expand and deepen the discussion on the theme of otherness. Moreover, the option for the poor does not guarantee that a practice with a colonialist approach will not be reproduced. Commenting on these inconsistencies where they should not exist, Paulo Freire says that "unfortunately, however, in this 'tale' of the 'banking' conception, revolutionary leaders often fall ...",[38] there are even some well-intentioned ones with good projects, but who do not represent the aspirations of that population.

Missiological Answers to the Situation of the "Poor"
David Hesselgrave (Paradigms in Conflict, p. 122)

Liberation Theology		Holistic Theology		Primacy Theology
Radical	**Revisionist**	**Moderate**	**Traditional**
The mission is to promote justice in society and to establish God's *Shalom* on earth.	The mission is to minister to society and individuals without dichotomising between the physical and the spiritual or the body and the soul.	The mission is to minister socially and spiritually to society and individuals, giving a certain priority to "evangelism".	The mission is firstly to make disciples in all nations. Other Christian ministries are good, but secondary and as support.

Traditional theology, in turn, reduces our entire mission in this world to a ransom of "souls for eternity".

Hesselgrave makes clear his position that the purpose of missiology is to fulfil the Great Commission. According to him, the effort to fulfil the *Missio Dei* came to be separated from obedience to the Great Commission of God. For this author, the church must be the centre of the mission and our whole mission is to obey the Great Commission, which he calls "mission of the Great Commission".

Despite doing interesting research on the main missionary conferences throughout history, Hesselgrave seems stuck in the dichotomous reasoning that accuses the theology of *Missio Dei* as leaving the missiology very open and thus greatly diluting the role of the Church. Like others, he mixes the concepts of evangelism and mission. The former fits into ecclesiology, but the latter cannot be imprisoned there. God is the centre of mission and allows the church to participate with him in his project.

Of the options advanced by the author, I have a tendency to identify better with what he calls "Holistic Revisionist Theology", although I do not fit into any of the possibilities presented in the book. I find his argument incomplete, for even in this one, the Church is at the centre, rather than considered simply a part of God's purpose for the world. Thinking from the standpoint of *Missio Dei* leads us to a more systemic theology because we engage in God's design for the world which contemplates the redemption of all of his creation and does not only focus on saving people to populate the sky; it helps us to break with the Enlightenment approach that departmentalized theology and reinforced the dualism so deeply rooted in evangelical thought.

The Lausanne Movement has already brought this agenda of the integrality of mission to the discussion agenda for decades, and in the third meeting, held in South Africa in 2010, the final document of the Congress reaffirmed the "commitment to the dynamic and integral exercise of all the dimensions of the mission to which God calls his whole church",[39] maintaining the theological vision that since 1974 in the Lausanne Pact has defined evangelization as "the whole church bringing the whole gospel to the whole world".[40]

Samuel Escobar, commenting on the conduct of this first event and its contents, summarizes that they expressed "a strong challenge to adopt a new form of missionary practice for world evangelization".[41] However, the discussion on missionary practice and how Integral Mission "would be earthed" did not sail through deeper waters. In the third meeting in Cape Town, the holistic dimension of the mission no longer shone as it had done in 1974, but was rather muted. Even so, it is still possible to register some isolated champions who persist in defending the banner of the integral gospel, although missionary practice predominantly continues to be colonialist.

We must also admit that this reflection on Integral Mission here in Brazil is carried out in a fragmented manner, guided by different theological schools, and this diversity produces a tendency in which the majority concentrates the discussion on the preaching of the gospel and social responsibility, leaving the agenda of the otherness and coloniality in the background. Generally, polarization comes down to these topics. And even understanding the mission as an enterprise that goes far beyond the reductionist conception of preaching to "bring souls to heaven", we find people in some of these sectors who are falling into the same trap as the Western model: contact with 'the other' starts with the assumption of superiority of the one who moves from their means to "help the poor" or "the different" and decide what is best for them.

The conception of mission as *Missio Dei* makes the vision more systemic, centralizes all the leadership in God, and makes theology less anthropocentric and more theocentric. The guiding light becomes greater, clearer and more comprehensive. And if the mission is God's, the Christian's homework is to be in touch with the signs of the times, to find out where the wind blows, to be sensitive to the Holy Spirit, who can guide the agenda and steer us to the divine priorities. It is to embody the mission of Jesus, who said, "As the Father has sent me, so have I sent you".[42] We have received a mission similar to his, given in the power of the Holy Spirit for love, giving, service and glorification of the Father.

For Comblin, love and the cross are intrinsically linked to mission, for "there was a cross because God resolved to save mankind by the pure force of love, without any form of imposition, punishment or embarrassment".[43] I believe that the Church has the task of giving continuity to this mission of the love of Jesus. And she must at all times be aware that the fulfilment of this role is her reason for existing.

Being daughters and sons of God, we co-operate with him in his project and also are a part of what he is doing in the universe. Roberto Zwetsch talks about this engagement in mission, affirming that "it is urgent to return to the idea that we are God's co-workers" (1 Cor. 3:9) in his *missio*, for good, justice and peace among people...".[44] We have his DNA and we get involved because his love constrains us and drives us to love his other creatures and not just to obey an ordinance stuck in the gospels. "Doing" out of "duty" trivializes and weakens mission, for if our mission commitment is based only on Jesus' command in Matthew 28, mission becomes an obligation rather than an act of love and grace.

The motivation is the glory of God and not an expectation of reward, or even fear of divine judgments and punishments. Engaging in God's project is to see 'the other' as God sees them, it is to relate on the basis of dialogicity and love of neighbour, as he did while he was here in Christ. Sharing the faith arises as a right won from mutual trust respect, and many times, from admiration.

Using a phrase I started to use among young people in lectures on God's mission – "God, do not leave me out of what the Lord is doing in the world" – some friends baptized this catchphrase as the "youthful version of the *Missio Dei*" and began to spread the idea on the internet. The expression is a prayer that recognizes that the engagement in so-called "missionary work" is not just a choice to leave your country to preach the gospel in another nation, but refers to a commitment of partnership and co-operation with what God is doing in the world. It is a decision to make a contribution in this "project of God" with what he knows and likes to do, always from the perspective of the glorification of God in the world. It is to opt for a lifestyle of living under the authority of Jesus Christ and relating to people wherever you are; this relationship is dialogical and loving, and not only preoccupied with distributing pamphlets or getting people to church. In it, "being" is more important than "doing".

In one of the socio-missionary projects developed by IBAB (Água Branca Baptist Church, São Paulo),[45] there is a partnership with YWAM (Youth with a Mission) at Morro do Borel, Rio de Janeiro. One of the activities we repeat constantly is beauty care for women, which is always a great success amongst the ladies and girls in the community. We have the support of a highly respected beauty salon in Rio de Janeiro, which participates with several aesthetics professionals, including the owner, who belongs to a city church. We have heard more than once that his employees claim that he treats the hair of a woman from the *morro* [poor districts on the hillsides in Rio de Janeiro] with the same excellence and affection that he dispenses to the madams [society ladies] who attend his salon. I have no doubt that with this project in Borel and his daily routine, he is participating in what God is doing in the world with his gifts and abilities. Several times, we have found women crying during their "beauty treatment", and the frequent question is almost always the same: "Why do you do this?".

Just like this entrepreneur, hundreds of excellent professionals who love God may never leave their Brazilian cities or wider Brazil to "do missions", but surely their lives have transmitted the love of God for the people who live with them.

Thinking of mission as "God's work" in the world also leads us to reflect on other concepts. Thus, being called to God's work is not necessarily a calling to be a pastor, priest or missionary, but to recognize one's part in the mission of God and strive to give one's contribution with one's gifts, talents and abilities, since every Christian is God-ordained. If the church is the Body of Christ on earth, every Christian has a purpose and a role to play. The Reformation already preached the universal priesthood of every believer, which also led to the idea of the responsibility of every Christian to serve God. Afterwards, Luther himself, because of events with the Anabaptists, retreated in his ideas, further tightening the doctrine which centralized service in the clergy. The subject is challenging, but we stop here now, because the theology of vocation would lead us to other issues which are not part of the central subject of this book.

Participating in God's mission gives us empathy for his purposes for humanity. To do so is to align our goals with his goals for the world. It is discovering our personal mission of life and work in harmony with God's purposes for the planet. It is an option for a lifestyle, not simply a decision to plant churches and "convert souls". An inexplicable love for the neighbour invades our being with a new feeling of diaconia [caring service]. Complying with programmes no longer satisfies us, because we want to interact with people. Making use of Alan Kreider's idea (diagram in chapter two) that Christendom should be something of the past, we propose a search for suitable ways of "doing mission" in post-Christendom, with a relational and decolonial practice, that is, a search done with missiology established in dialogicity. See a comparative table of different mission models on the next page.

In an interview with the Brazilian Baptist World Mission Board, Pastor Ed René, commenting on the reductionism we have discussed, urged the reader to go well beyond this managerial goal and rescue the notion that the disciples and the churches are "salt of the earth and light world", announcing and manifesting in history the greatest of the kingdom of God, which will be consummated in eternity. More than an obtuse vision that evaluates results quantitatively, we are challenged to be Christ for our generation, established in the order and desire of Jesus Christ contained in the biblical text of the Gospel of John 20:21.

Mission Models – Comparative Table (Analzira Nascimento)

	Period	Purpose of the Mission	Text	Project	Motivation	Method	Logic
Pre-Christendom	Until the 3rd Century	To transmit the love of God	Acts 4:20 Rom 5:8	The Church of Christ	The love of God	Relational	Sharing the love of God
Christendom	4th – 17th Centuries	Christianization	Luke 14:23	Catholicity	Dominion/ expansion	Coercion	Uniformization/ control
	18th –and 19th centuries	Civilizationist	Acts 16: 9	Protestant	Reproduce model culture	Transplant culture/ educate	Uniformization/ expansion
	20th Century	Conversionist	Matt 28:20	Evangelical	Saving souls/ Planting churches	Accountable (manageable)	Fulfil programs
Post-Christendom (Decolonial Missiology)	21st Century	Dialogicity	John 20:21	Church of Christ	Glory of God/ love of God	Dialogical/ relational	Participate in the Missio Dei

We can affirm that evangelization is not only the proclamation of the gospel. Written or spoken preaching does not always communicate effectively. As we could see in the example cited in the introduction about the experiences of war in Angola, when people from the Huambo church refused to leave the city in combat, but confirmed their solidarity by providing relief to the wounded, government structures were destroyed, guerrillas controlled the city and doctors fled, but that decision to remain was emblematic:

> communicating much more with attitudes than with speeches the truth of the gospel of Jesus Christ, which were of great comfort for the population. The presence of the Baptist community together with the population in the most difficult moments of the war gave it credibility before the government, International NGOs and the UN.[46]

Therefore, to live an authentic Christian faith at all times and in every place, and not only "do missions" by choosing an ecclesiastical career or engaging in occasional short-term missionary activities should be the primary goal of every Christian. The reason for a Christian's life and the reason for the existence of the Church are for the glory of God in this world. The meaning of life is to participate in God's plan for humanity, to fulfil the purpose for which we were created.

People were drawn to Christianity in the first century not because of their efficient evangelistic methods, or through their elaborate theology and impeccable liturgies, not even by the construction of sumptuous temples, but they were sensitized and drawn to faith in Christ through Christians and Christian communities which had a challenging lifestyle and viscerally lived the teachings of Jesus. Seeing the world from a Christian perspective was a living reality in its midst.

Concerned about maintaining a dialogue with neighbouring peoples, the early Christians were not "chattering" about their faith, but the Church grew rapidly because the Christians lived attractively, drawing people to the faith. Kreider states that at that time they were doing so naturally, but in Christendom this stopped being natural in order to be missionary. The celebrations were of the worship of God and preparing Christians to live an attractive daily life, but in Christendom the worship had a focus on the conversion of those who were "outsiders".

Hugo Assmann, writing about the missionary dimension of the Church, argues that there is a need to redefine mission. The Church must overcome the merely "salvationist" sense of her mission, get out of her "ghetto seclusion", and take a new stand.

The mission of the Church is understood by Bosch as an indispensable dimension of the Christian faith and that, "at its deepest level, its purpose is to transform the reality that surrounds it. Mission, in this perspective, is that dimension of our faith that refuses to accept reality as it is and aims to transform it".[47]

Within this transformational conjuncture, missionary action can play a preponderant role in this critical moment of humanity, when we live through the current disenchantment with the socio-political systems, and how dominant systems fail to see the poorest and most vulnerable parts of regions and countries with low HDI. As Todorov suggests, this action might be a bridge-builder and a promoter of the "cross-cultural dialogue that characterizes our time [...], a dialogue in which no one has the last word, in which none of the voices reduces 'the other' to *status* of a mere object...".[48] In that same text, Todorov underscores the need for us to review our conception of 'the other' and to work for a culture of cultures of – and why not? – for a frontier culture.

We must draw lessons from pioneer incursions in the past. We agree that "the church needs to learn from history and prepare its missionaries well, to understand their task of cultivating a native Christianity contextualized in the receiving culture",[49] not only living among them and like them, but having a relationship with them on the basis of equality, gaining trust and the right to be heard.

With a model of missionary practice articulating a dynamic intercultural dialogue, it will be possible to work for a frontier consciousness that acts using a new logic which would be capable of making a break from silencing monoculturalism, an *incarnational* missionary action, which has the courage and humility to revise its methodologies and the willingness to recommence and eliminate all the colonialist remnants of its model. Thus, missiology will not have an exclusive focus on the contents of the missionary message, but also in the role of the messenger. Roland Muller, in his book, talks about the importance of each missionary respecting and analyzing the local culture incorporating some practices in their daily life,

> since when we foreigners enter a cross-cultural context, we need to be sensitive to cultural issues, and realize that it takes time to be accepted as a valid messenger. Relationships need to be built and lessons need to be learned.[50]

This can be the choice for an exchange, cooperation, solidarity and, above all, sharing life among peoples.

The Church of the South, having the experience of a colonized victim, can arise with a prophetic voice and relevant action. The essential thing is not how much action she undertakes, but what kind of action she performs, as Samuel Escobar said. Depending on the course to be taken, mission can regain its purpose, redefining its real motivations, and certainly find its special place. In this search for meaning, mission can present the vision of the kingdom of God, encouraging interdependence and, according to Sung, proclaiming the possibility of a new way of living and "the search for a new meaning of life, a more human meaning, which presupposes and at the same time is made up of a new way of seeing and comprehending life and the reality which surrounds us".[51] This is what Bosch calls a polemical tension with the system of this world. And it will be here that this Church on the edge, from the periphery, can play a key role in paradigm transition and operationalization of the *new way of thinking and doing.*

It can encourage an activism working for a frontier culture. The church carries out a mission *with* 'the others' and not *for* 'the others'. Reviewing its motivations, the church can stop reproducing an anti-mission and participate in the *Missio Dei* respecting the agenda and the 'house of the other'.

Conclusion

Globalization has allowed for greater proximity among peoples who were previously isolated from each other, because the speed with which information is moving and circulating has massively facilitated conditions of greater tolerance between groups, and today it is possible to carry out projects in partnership in different regions of the world, and to share cultural productions, values, ideas and customs, in a much more efficient and agile way.

However, the contact between different cultures has often represented an annihilation of autochthonous cultures by other hegemonic ones. Some dominant societies have culturally cannibalized other social segments that they considered less expressive and poorer, or simply because they were different. This is a thought that is shared by Boaventura de Sousa Santos, in holding that this meeting caused an epistemicide [killing of knowledge systems] because it was a one-way street and the predominant monocultures destroyed alternative knowledge. He exemplifies this when remembering that Western culture and modernity imposed a colonial contact that was silencing and contemptuous. Therefore today,

> when we want to try a new discourse or intercultural theory, we face a problem: there are oppressed aspirations that are not predictable because they were considered improbable after centuries of oppression. The dialogue is not possible simply because people do not know how to speak: not because they have nothing to say but because their aspirations are unutterable.[1]

This type of meeting was characterized as imperialist and "silencing" because the "weaker" side did not have the chance to sit at the same table and present their ideas, proposals and wishes. Today, the great challenge that remains for our generation is to articulate possibilities that make the "silence speak", thus breaking the cycle which continues to reproduce silencing, which is not an easy task.

Enrique Dussel also denounces this arrogance of Western thought and reveals how modernities, from the 16th century, built a conception of knowledge that subordinated other epistemologies. For the writer, the idea of Western superiority presupposes the colonial difference, which transforms differences into values.

In the midst of criticism of all forms of sociocultural subjugation, especially disrespect for otherness, an important lesson emerges for missiology: the possibility of reviewing its approaches in the models of missionary practice, since the past shows us that, predominantly, there was no exchange, no reciprocity, no interculturality in mission undertakings, on the contrary, very often on these occasions the contact is portrayed as imperialist and colonialist.

The research which gave rise to this book allowed us to see how, in the course of history, at times the missionary movement's journey took steps which facilitated its departure from the initial purpose of Christianity. Chapter two showed how institutionalization and hierarchy consequently prepared the configuration of the missionary model that would later receive the seal of approval from strong colonialist expansionist movements.

The Enlightenment comes into play to make its great contribution, as I described in chapter three, to shape the North American model that became the matrix of the dominant model in Protestant mission practice with its ideas of Western superiority and rationality. Their beliefs in progress helped to leverage Christian expansion and sow the ideology of Manifest Destiny, which in turn came to determine the type of approach in missionary action in their encounters with 'the other': those who consider that they with their superior culture are sent to help the poor and decide what is best for them.

We also recall how much puritanism and pietism, which encouraged contempt for "earthly things", influenced the process of forming the basis of conservative evangelical thought. They contributed to reinforce this dualistic heritage in the missionary model, which insists on only prioritizing kerygmatic strategy, because to them what really matters is the "salvation of souls", a concept that also gives a seal of approval to the "concealment of 'the other'".

The conversionist mission and its predecessor, the civilizational vision found fertile ground in the countries of the South colonized by the North until the 20th century. Now, in the third millennium, in a world that has undergone significant changes and lives a paradigmatic socio-cultural and epistemological crisis, missionary action with its strategies also shows clear signs of exhaustion. It is precisely with this crisis that chapter one opened the text and chapter four brings a proposal for a re-encounter with a dialogical model.

The missionary practice currently reigning in the Protestant world continues reproducing the Eurocentric colonialist logic of domination that reinforces the denial of the identity of 'the other' and it reduces it to an object, so this subject also gives us a reflection on our true motivation in the search for new adherents for our Christian group. With the cooling of the ideology of Manifest Destiny, "the elect" no longer need to look after and save the world. It is now enough to preach the gospel to "to win souls" and "populate the sky". This missiology accumulates privileged quantitative results, causing 'the other' to continue being invisible and the gives importance to the fulfilment of the aims. For this reason, we have perceived that some more conservative agencies are afraid of those who want to live mission integrally.

Missionaries aligned with this dominant model rarely care about the complete fulfilment of human beings. There is little interest in their complete well-being, after all, the mission of the Christian in this world is to gather souls for heaven. The body can suffer because the physical world has no value. Some have abolished continuing education projects for nationals because this business of higher education is for Westerners. Discarding some content and passing on formulas to people give them the feeling of fulfilling their duty as Christians.

The obsession with manageability, with its methods and schemes, diverted the focus of the relationship with people to the fulfilment of church programmes and organizations. The feeling of superiority that was infused into the model of mission continues to lead many missionaries to believe that they are the ones who know the best projects for the culture to which they will be sent and continue to feel themselves as their "saviours".

We find that it is necessary to listen to understand, and to comprehend, to gain conditions for dialogue. The one who feels "superior" thinks they know everything, and so for them communication follows a one-way path. Their arrogance, although full of piety, limits their vision and prevents them from discovering the riches of other worldviews. If we do not listen to the people, we do not have much to say to them. We therefore need be attentive and be cautious with silencing practices. It needs humility to admit that 'the other' also has something to say and not to label differences as inferiority.

When we do not listen, we invade 'the other's house', we enjoy 'their hospitality', and use people as a trampoline to achieve our goals. It is a "cultural invasion, as in all other forms of anti-dialogical action, the invaders are the authors and the actors in the process, their subject; those who have been invaded, their objects. The invaders model; those who are invaded are modelled".[2] When we impose our vision of the world, we threaten to deteriorate its originality and curb its potentialities and creativities.

If we recognize the deviations in history and recover a systemic approach that recognizes the *Missio Dei* as the central project of Christianity, it will be possible to construct a multicultural counter-hegemonic concept in Christian mission. Mission ventures are no longer mere human initiatives but are recognized as part of God's work in the world. Ecclesio-centric logic reduces the primordial purpose of mission in Christian actions to spread Christianity, diverting the focus from the leading role of God who works and acts in this world and invites every Christian to participate in what he is doing in the universe to fulfil his purposes.

Can we draw lessons from imperialist experiences? We realize that "today's church, in fulfilling its missionary task, must take this danger seriously. Did we really learn from history? It is easy to reproduce the errors of past missionaries and to implant a version of Christianity based on the culture of the missionary".[3] Very often, our "adaptation" is just a cover. It is just a passport to approach other peoples and communities, but the conception is still colonialist because we consider "these people who are so different" to be inferior.

If the church learned from history, it would know that it needs to be attentive to the signs of the times and sensitive in their interactions with 'the other', seeking a dialogical relationship and, to continue having the initial relevance and fulfilling the purpose for which it exists, it needs to be flexible to change and to look for adaptions.

Convened by the representatives of the Lausanne Movement in Brazil and supported by three more organizations, some evangelical leaders gathered in November 2012 to reflect on the question "what are the main reasons that prevent the Brazilian church from sending more transcultural missionaries"? The group admitted that most churches still confuse the mission of God with missionary endeavours of the local church, also recognizing that missions have become a department of the church and not the reason for its existence as church. One of the points deserving of discussion was the realization that "the leadership of the churches and missionary agencies do not know how to deal with the changes that are taking place on the world stage and affect the way of doing missions".[4] There is an obvious mismatch between the approaches and methodologies employed and the demands of the new times.

Bosch reminds us of a truth we must not forget: the need to be constantly *becoming*, because:

> This whole study is based on the premise that the definition of mission is an ongoing process of sifting, testing, reformulating and discarding. This means that mission must be understood as an activity that transforms reality and, simultaneously, that there is a constant need for the mission to transform itself.[5]

Therefore, this thesis reinforces the urgency of missiology including in its agenda the reflection on otherness, since the model that prevails in missionary action suffers from exhaustion and has been characterized as catechetical, it cannot listen to 'the other', and its greatest concern is the fulfilment of programmes. It could define as one of its aims to work for the construction of frontier thinking which rescues dialogical practice and promotes co-existence between those who are different to each other, guiding its evangelistic approach to stop being one of "banking" and therefore recover its strong relational and incarnational identity. It could also participate in the construction of a multicultural approach which would reject the vertical approach and its hegemonic silencing contact. This attitude would combat the reproduction of a "single story", which insists on interpreting other cultures from one's own worldview. And, obviously, it would considerably reduce the stereotypes created because of our insecurities in the encounter with those who are different and their differences. Émile Léonard also referred to this situation commenting on the fact that people visiting a culture judge or speak precipitately about the reality of the new place or its costumes "without a profound understanding of the country, [something] which still happens constantly in our days, with priests, who after a brief speaking trip, expound in other countries their hasty opinions as being definitive".[6]

It is important to think of mission and otherness recovering a relational dialogical approach because the world has changed definitively. New problems emerge in the world agenda. Hoping that missiology will be responsible for changes in missionary practice is to run the risk of remaining in rhetoric and abstractions, because [the entity] missiology does not construct models by decree. The purpose of this book is speak to people, men and women, young people and children and partners in ministry, to put ourselves into the hands of God to collaborate with him in what he wants to do in the world.

The Southern Church, as a colonized victim, should no longer reproduce past mistakes which promote an anti-mission, but seek alternatives that neutralize the colonizing matrix that reigns in the missionary model. In some European countries, theologians and thinkers are writing books on emerging paradigms and possibilities for mission in post-Christendom. And Brazil, in a special way, needs to be attentive, drawing lessons, and humbly finding its role on the world stage, taking care not to be a new Christian empire.

> Sign the road to mark the way home.
> Find a good map.
> Study the road conditions.
> The exit is the way back.
>
> - Jeremiah 31:21, *The Message*

Notes

In this book, the translators' and editors' comments or suggestions are made between [ ] brackets.

Introduction

1. Wars in Angola – 1961, movements of resistance to the colonial Portuguese regime began an armed struggle, these continued until 1975 when they achieved independence for Angola. From that year onwards, two of the movements did not agree about a transitional government and the signed protocols, beginning a new conflict, between MPLA, the USSR backed governing party, and UNITA, a movement assisted by the United States in opposition to the Marxist-Leninist regime. The war only ended in 2002 with the death of Jonas Savimbi, the leader of the guerrilla group, and the signing of peace agreements.
2. NASCIMENTO, Analzira. *Crise e esperança* [*Crisis and Hope*]; the pastoral praxis of the Baptist Church in the Angolan war, São Paulo: 235 page dissertation for Master's Degree in Religious Sciences at UMESP [Methodist University in São Paulo,] p. 154.
3. BOSCH, David. *Missão transformadora; mudanças de paradigma in the theology of mission*, São Leopoldo: Sinodal, 2002, p. 609. This South African missiologist analyzes the conferences which influenced missionary movements and the understanding of mission. At the Willingen Conference (1952), MARTYRIA (an all-embracing concept) = Kerygma + Diaconia + Koinonia, was adopted. [For the English version of this book see David J. Bosch, *Transforming Mission, Paradigm Shifts in Theology of Mission*, New York: Orbis Books, 1991, bearing in mind the page numbers will be different.]
4. Paulo Freire refers to "banking education" as a methodology in which the student is simply a receptacle into which the contents "are emptied". The posture is passive, it is sufficient to memorize or to repeat the information. There is no dialogicity.
5. BOSCH, *Missão transformadora*, p. 617.
6. SANTOS, Boaventura de Sousa. *Renovar a teoria crítica e reinventar a emancipação social*, São Paulo: Boitempo, 2007. p. 25.
7. SANTOS, Boaventura de Sousa. *A crítica da razão indolente; contra o desperdício da experiência* [*Criticism of lazy reasoning, against wastage of experience.*] São Paulo: Cortez. 2009. p. 83.

Chapter 1

1. FREIRE, Paulo. *Pedagogy do oprimido.* São Paulo: Paz e Terra, 2007. p. 66. [This book was first published in Portuguese in 1968, and the first English translation appeared in 1970. Many subsequent editions have appeared since.]

2. SANTOS, Boaventura de Sousa. *A gramática do tempo; para uma nova cultura política,* São Paulo: Cortez, 2006. p. 25.

3. KUHN, Thomas. *A estrutura da revoluções científicas.* São Paulo: Perspectiva, 2011. p. 118. [This book was first published in English by University of Chicago Press in 1962, and is still available.]

4. KUHN, *A estrutura da revoluções científicas*, p. 91.

5. KUHN, *A estrutura da revoluções científicas*, p. 134.

6. BOSCH, *Missão transformadora*, p. 231.

7. CERTEAU, Michel de. *A cultura no plural,* Campinas, São Paulo: Papirus Editora, 2005. p. 25. [English version *Culture in the Plural*, published in 1974 – still available.]

8. DE CERTEAU, *A cultura no plural*, p. 29.

9. TOURAINE, Alain. *Um novo paradigma; para compreender o mundo de hoje* [*A new paradigm; to understand today's world.*] Petrópolis: Vozes, 2011. p. 12.

10. SUNG, Jung Mo. *Educar para reencantar a vida.* [*Educate to re-enchant life*] Petrópolis: Vozes, 2006. p. 112.

11. SANTOS, Boaventura de Sousa. *A gramática do tempo;* para uma nova cultura política. São Paulo: Cortez, 2006. p. 28.

12. SANTOS, Boaventura de Sousa. *Renovar a teoria crítica e reinventar a emancipação social.* São Paulo: Boitempo, 2007. p. 55.

13. SUESS, Paulo, Ed. *Culturas e evangelização; a unidade da razão evangélica na multiplicidade de suas vozes:pressupostos, desafios e comprimissos.* São Paulo: Edições Loyola, 1991. p. 112.

14. *Missiologia* – Samuel Escobar defines missiology as "an interdisciplinary study to understand missionary action. It looks at the missionary facts from the perspective of biblical studies, theology, history and social sciences [...] A missiological study gives the observer a comprehensive structure in order to look at reality in a critical way. Missiology is a critical reflection on praxis, in the light of the Word of God. It is possible to say that, starting with this consideration, a significant part of the writings of the apostle Paul is missiological in its nature". (ESCOBAR, Samuel. "Missiologia evangélica; olhando para o futuro na virada do século". [Evangelical Missiology looking to the future at the turn of the century.] In: William D. Taylor, Ed. *Missiologia global para o século XXI; a consulta de Foz do Iguaçu.* Londrina: Descoberta, 2001. p. 145).

15. BOSCH, *Missão transformadora*, p. 617.

16. HESSELGRAVE, David. *Paradigms in conflict; 10 key questions in Christian missions today.* Grand Rapids, MI: Kregel Academic Publications, 2005. p. 342.

17. KREIDER, Alan. "Beyond Bosch; the early church and the Christendom shift". *International Bulletin of Missionary Research,* Overseas Ministries Studies Center 29(2), (April 2005). p. 66. For the author, pre-Christianity lasts until Constantine, which is also is the mark of the beginning of Christianity. Post-Christianity begins with the crisis of the western epistemological and sociocultural paradigm.

18. Bosch affirms that "the commitment to Social Reform was the consequence of the enthusiasm inherited from revivals [...] the evangelical unity shaped by the Awakenings was about to disintegrate; the vast river of classic evangelicalism divided into a delta, with shallower currents emphasizing ecumenism and social

renewal, to the left, and confessional orthodoxy and evangelism, to the right. At the beginning of the 20th century, the first segment evolved into the social gospel and the second into fundamentalism". BOSCH, *Missão transformadora*, p. 344.

19. BOSCH, *Missão transformadora*, p.427.
20. BOSCH, *Missão transformadora*, p. 362.
21. BOSCH, *Missão transformadora*, p. 334.
22. TODOROV, Tzvetan. *A Conquista da América; a questão do Outro*. São Paulo: Martins Fontes, 2003. p. 278. [cf *The conquest of America: the Question of the Other*, translated from the French into English in 1984, and published by Harper Rowe, New York.]
23. DUSSEL, Enrique. 1492 – *O encobrimento do outro; a origem do mito da modernidade*. Petrópolis: Vozes: 1993. p. 31.
24. A Catholic monk who during his life became a Dominican. He was a prophetic voice of denunciation, cultivation (of the land), and salaried labour. With the use of slave labour, the system degenerated (GALMÉS, Lorenzo. *Bartolomeu de Las Casas; Defensor dos direitos dos índios*, São Paulo: Edições Paulinas, 1991. p. 12.)
28. GALMÉS, *Bartolomeu de Las Casas*, p.190.
29. HOONAERT, Eduardo. *Histórias da Igreja no Brasil, ansaio de interpretação a partir do povo*. [*History of the Church in Brazil, starting with the people*,] Petrópolis: Vozes, 1992. p. 27.
30. Bosch speaks about the sending of the Son by the Father and of the Spirit sent by the Father and by the Son. He develops a chapter to expound this theory of the *Missio Dei* which was expanded in the sense of including one more "movement": "Father, Son and Holy Spirit sending the Church into the world".
31. ANTONE, Hope S. "Towards a new paradigm in the concepts of mission". *Theologies and Cultures*. 5,(2), (December 2008). p. 88.
32. DE CERTEAU, Michel. *Invenção do cotidiano; artes de fazer*. Petrópolis: Vozes, 1996. pp. 97 and 208.
33. NEILL, Stephen. *História das missões*. São Paulo: Edições Vida Nova, 1997. p. 118. [cf Stephen Neill, *A History of Christian Missions*. London: Penguin Books, 1964.]
34. SUESS, Paulo, Ed. *Culturas e evangelização; a unidade da razão evangélica in the multiplicity of its voices: presuppositions, challenges and commitments*. São Paulo: Edições Loyola, 1991. p. 111.
35. BOSCH, *Missão transformadora*, p.378.
36. SANTOS, Boaventura de Sousa. *Reinovar a teoria crítica e reinventar a emancipação social*. São Paulo: Boitempo, 2007. p. 59.
37. *BETANCOURT, Raul Fornet. Religião e interculturalidade.* [*Religion and interculturality*] São Leopoldo: Nova Harmonia/Sinodal, 2007. p. 15.
38. SUESS, *Culturas e evangelização*, p. 109.
39. SUESS, *Culturas e evangelização*, p. 105.
40. SANTOS, Boaventura de Sousa. *Semear outras soluções: os caminhos da biodiversidade e dos conhecimentos rivais*. Rio de Janeiro: Civilização Brasileira. 2005. p. 28.
41. BOSCH, *Missão transformadora*, p. 617.
42. EITEL, Keith E. "On becoming missional: interacting with Charles van Engen". In: David J HESSELGRAVE and Ed STETZER, Eds. *Mission Shift; global mission issues in the third millennium*. Nashville: B&H Academic, 2010, p. 38. (author's translation).
43. COSTAS, Orlando. *Compromiso y mission.* [*Commitment and Mission*] San José. Costa Rica: Editorial Caribe, Colección CELEP, 1979. p.70.

44. PADDILLA, René. *Missão Integral; O reino de Deus e a igreja.* [*Integral Mission: The kingdom of God and the church*]. Viçosa: Ultimato, 2014.
45. *Terceira Igreja* (Third Church) – a concept adopted by Samuel Escobar to refer to the Church of the Third Millennium. The argument explains that in the first thousand years in the history of Christianity, the leadership of the Eastern Church predominated and in the second millennium the Western Church undertook the evangelization of the world. The emerging Third Church, which appeared in this new millennium, is the Church of the Southern Hemisphere. ESCOBAR, Samuel. "The global scene at the turn of the century". In: TAYLOR, William D., Ed. *Missiologia Global para o século XXI* [Global missiology for the 21st century] the Foz do Iguaçu consultation. Londrina: Descoberta, 2001. p. 49.
46. ESCOBAR, Samuel. "O cenário global na virada do século". [the global scene at the turn of the century] In: TAYLOR, William D., Ed. *Missiologia para o século XXI: a consulta de Foz do Iguaçu.* Londrina: Descoberta, 2001. p. 49.
47. ESCOBAR, Samuel. "Missiologia evangélica; olhando para o futuro na virada do século". In: TAYLOR, William D., Ed. *Missiologia global para o século XXI; a consulta de Foz do Iguaçu.* Londrina: Descoberta. 2001. p. 159.
48. MELIÁ, Bartolomeu. "Culturas indígenas e evangelização; desafios para uma missão libertadora" [Indigenous cultures and evangelism: challenges for a liberating mission]. In: SUESS, *Culturas e evangelização,* p. 81. The author analyzes the records made on 11 October 1492 in the diary of Columbus. According to this, on this first day, Columbus metaphorically represents the essential question of the Christianizing of the indigenous cultures: the question of the poor (*everything they took and gave),* from the pagan (*they did not have a sect*) and the barbarians *(they had to learn how to speak).*
49. KREIDER, Alan. "Beyond Bosch; the early church and the Christendom shift". *International Bulletin of Missionary Research,* Overseas Ministries Studies Center. 29(2), (April 2005). p. 67.

Chapter 2

1. KREIDER, Alan. "Beyond Bosch; the early church and the Christendom shift". *International   Bulletin of Missionary Research,* Overseas Ministries Studies Center. 29(2), (April 2005).   The explanations which follow are based on the passage from pages 62-66.
2. JENKINS, Philip. *A próxima cristandade; a chegada do cristianismo global.* Rio de Janeiro: Record, 2004. p. 18. [cf *The Next Christendom: the coming of global Christianity*]. New York: Oxford University Press, 2002.]
3. According to Roger Bastide, the word "dogma" had two meanings amongst the Greeks: 1) the collection of decisions made by civil or religious authorities; 2) between philosophers, doctrinal summary or of a certain teaching. It was a decision of the authority and marks the limits between the Church and heresy (BASTIDE, Roger, *Elementos de sociologia religiosa.* Trans. Prócoro Valesques Filho. São Bernado do Campo: Instituto Ecumênico de Pós Graduação em Ciências da Religião – Núcleo de São Bernado do Campo, 1990. p. 45. [cf Roger Bastide, *Social Origins of Religion,* Minneapolis, MN: University of Minnesota Press, 2003.]
4. KÜNG, Hans. *Religiões do mundo; em busca dos pontos comuns.* Campinas: Versus Editora, 2005. p. 224. [cf Hans Kühn, *Christianity and World Religions: Paths of dialogue with Islam, Hinduism and Buddhism*].
5. KÜNG, Hans. *Religiões do mundo,* p 249.

6. BOSCH, David. *Missão transformadora: mudanças de paradigma na teologia da Missão.* São Leopoldo: Sinodal, 2002. p. 255. [For the English version of this book, see David J. Bosch, *Transforming Mission, Paradigm Shifts in Theology of Mission,* New York: Orbis Books, 1991, although bear in mind that the page numbers will be different].

7. BOSCH, *Missão transformadora,* p. 249.

8. BOSCH, *Missão transformadora,* p. 268.

9. MILLER, Darrow. *Vocação; escreva sua assinatura no Universo. [Vocation; write your membership in the universe*] Curitiba: Instituto e Publicações Transforma / DNA Brasil, 2012. p. 40.

10. BOSCH, *Missão transformadora,* p. 286.

11. GONZÁLEZ, Justo L, and ORLANDI, Carlos C. *História do movimento missionário. [History of the missionary movement]* São Paulo: Hagnos, 2008. p. 103.

12. Indulgences – the church gave pardon for sins and the certainty of "paradise" in return for payment or the giving of service.

13. BOSCH, *Missão transformadora,* p. 177.

14. DUSSEL, Enrique. *Desintegración de la cristianidad colonial y liberación. [Disintegration of Colonial Christianity and Liberation],* Salamanca: Ediciones Sigueme, 1977. p. 49.

15. DUSSEL, *Desintegración de la cristianidad colonial y liberación,* p. 69.

16. HOORNAERT, Eduardo. *História da igreja no Brasil; ensaio de interpretação a partir do povo. [History of the church in Brazil: an interpretive essay from the perspective of the people]* Petrópolis: Vozes. 1992. p.113.

17. DUSSEL, Enrique. *1492 – O encobrimento do outro; a origen do mito da modernidade. [The hiding of the other: the origin of the myth of modernity].* Petrópolis: Vozes. 1993, p. 113. [cf *The Invention of the Americas,* Book 1, Continuum Intl Publications Group, 1995].

18. DUSSEL, Enrique. *Ética de la liberación en la edad de la globalización y de la exclusion.* Madrid: Trotta, 2002. p. 51. [cf DUSSEL, Enrique, *Ethics of Liberation in Age of Globalization.* Durham, NC: Duke University Press: 2013].

19. TODOROV, Tzvetan. *A conquista da América; a questão do outro.* São Paulo: Martins Fontes, 2003. p. 7. [cf *The Conquest of America: the Question of the Other,* translated from the French into English in 1984, and published by Harper Rowe, New York.]

20. Jean de Léry was a member of a French group which attempted to establish itself in Rio de Janeiro, in 1555, led by Nicolau Durand de Villegagnon. The French wanted to construct a French Antarctic in Brazil and in their midst were some Huguenots – the name given to protestants in France – who joined the group in 1557. One of the objectives of the expedition was to organize a type of Calvinist "refuge" for Protestants who were being persecuted in Europe. The initiative was part of the rush of the great European powers to secure power and which did not look for any missionary contact with the indigenous peoples. Their accounts have become valuable sources for the interpretation of the "spirit of the age".

21. DE CERTEAU, Michel. *A escrita da historia.* Rio de Janeiro: Forense Universitária, 2008. p. 217. [cf *The Writing of History,* New York: Columbia University Press. 1992.]

22. TODOROV. Tzvetan. *Nós e os outros; a reflexão francesa sobre a diversidade humana.* Rio de Janeiro: Zahar, 1993. p. 21.

23. QUIJANO, Anibal. "Coloniality of power, eurocentrism, and social classification".
    In: *Coloniality at Large*; Latin America and the postcolonial debate. Durham, NC:
    Duke University Press, 2008. p. 182.
24. LÉVI-STRAUSS, Claude. *Raça e história.* [Race and History], UNESCO: 1952. p.
    17.
25. Paul Hiebert, a Christian anthropologist defines *culture* as "more or less integrated
    systems of ideas, feelings, values and their associated standards of behavior and
    products, shared by a group of people who organize it and regulates what is thought,
    felt and done." HIEBERT, Paul, *O evangelho e a diversidade das culturas.* [The
    gospel and the diversity of cultures] São Paulo: Edições Vida Nova, 2001. p. 30.
26. For Clifford Geertz, culture "denotes a standard of meanings historically
    transmitted, incorporated as symbols, a system of inherited concepts expressed in
    symbolic terms by which human beings communicate, perpetuate, and develop their
    knowledge and activities in relation to life." GEERTZ, Clifford. *A interpretação das
    culturas.* Rio de Janeiro: LTC Editora, 1989. p. 103. [cf *The Interpretation of
    Cultures,* Clifford Geertz, Basic Books, New York, 1973.]
27. GUIMARÃES ROCHA, Everado. *O que é etnocentrismo.* [*What is ethnocentrism?*]
    São Paulo: Brasiliense. 1987. p. 7.
28. TODOROV, Tzvetan, *O medo dos bárboros; para além do choque das civilizações.*
    Petrópolis: Vozes, 2010. p. 24 [cf *The fear of the barbarians,* Polity Press. 2010.]
29. TODOROV, *O medo dos bárboros,* p. 26.
30. TODOROV, *O medo dos bárboros,* p. 34.
31. SANTOS, Boaventura de Sousa. *A gramática do tempo; para uma nova cultura
    política.* São Paulo: Cortez, 2006. p. 25.
32. SANTOS, *A crítica da razão indolente; contra o desperdício da experiência.* São
    Paulo: Cortez, 2009. p. 30.
33. VAINFAS, Ronaldo. *Economia e sociedade na América esponhola.* Rio de Janeiro.
    Edições Graal, 1984. p. 40.
34. HOORNAERT, *História da igreja no Brasil,* p.156.
35. RICHARD, Pablo. *Morte das cristandades e nascimento da igreja.* São Paulo:
    Edições Paulinas, 1982. p. 40.
36. HENDERSON, Lawrence. *A igreja em Angola.* Lisboa: Editorial Além Mar, 1990.
    p. 40. The document or 'bull' became known as *Romanus Pontifex* and gave three
    essential rights to Portugal: "1st: Only the monarch could present the names for
    bishops and other ecclesiastical positions to be filled by the Vatican; 2nd: Only the
    missionaries who had been sent or recognised by the monarchs could evangelise in
    the region of the ecclesiastical Patronage; 3rd: the monarch could take the initiative
    to proceed to alter the territories covered by the Patronages, for example the creation
    of new diocese, the relations with Rome, the establishment of convents and
    monasteries etc. However, the Patronage imposed certain obligations on Portugal:
    1st: To construct, repair, conserve the church buildings, monasteries and diocesan
    residences; 2nd:To support the clerics financially. 3rd: To nominate workers in
    sufficient numbers for the celebration of worship and for pastoral work; 4th: To
    provide the indispensable things needed for the running of the churches such as
    church furniture, ornaments, vestments, clerical robes and ceremonial table-ware".
37. CHANDA, Nayan. *Sem fronteira; os comerciantes, missionários, aventureiros e
    soldados que moldaram a globalização.* [*Without frontier; the merchants,
    missionaries, adventurers, and soldiers who shaped globalization.*] Rio de Janeiro:
    Record, 2011. p. 185.
38. BOSCH, *Missão transformadora,* p. 280.
39. VAINFAS, *Economia e sociedade na América esponhola,* p. 92.

40. HOORNAERT, *História da igreja no Brasil,* p. 34.
41. HOORNAERT, *História da igreja no Brasil,* p. 157.
42. Mercenários – Religious group from the Mercês Order, founded by S. Pedro Nolasco (1180 - 1256), a French monastic order, for the redemption of Christian slaves in the hands of the Moors, in Spain (*Novo Dicionário Aurélio da Língua Portuguesa.* 2nd ed. Rio de Janeiro: Editora Fronteira, 1994).
43. HOORNAERT, *História da igreja no Brasil,* p. 37.
44. VAINFAS, *Economia e sociedade na América esponhola,* p. 92.
45. RICHARD, *Morte das cristandades e nascimento da igreja,* p. 42.
46. HOORNAERT, *História da igreja no Brasil,* p. 38.
47. HOORNAERT, *História da igreja no Brasil,* p. 408.
48. HOORNAERT, *História da igreja no Brasil,* p. 410.
49. HOORNAERT, *História da igreja no Brasil,* p. 29.

Chapter 3

1. MENDONÇA, Antonio Gouvêa. *O celeste porvir; a inserção do protestantismo no Brasil.* [*The Heavenly Future: the insertion of Protestantism in Brazil*]. São Paulo: Edusp, 2008. p. 28.
2. Anabaptists – the group is thought to be one of the manifestations of XVI Century Protestantism. At present, there are various Baptist groups who identify themselves as being independent of Luther's Reformation. They radicalized the idea of the universal priesthood of every Christian, without territorial limits or restrictions to ordination to the ministry. They preached the separation between church and the state, "personal conversion repentance, which are symbolized and proclaimed by baptism." (GONZÁLEZ, Justo L. *Uma história do pensamento cristão; da reforma protestante ao século 20.* [*A History of Christian Thought: from the Protestant Reformation to the 20th Century.*] São Paulo: Cultura Cristã, 2004. p. 98.
3. NEILL, Stephen. *História das missões.* São Paulo: Edições Vida Nova, 1997. p. 225. [cf Stephen Neill, *A History of Christian Missions* Penguin Books, 1964].
4. GONZÁLEZ, *Uma história do pensamento cristão,* p. 104.
5. BOSCH, *Missão transformadora,* p. 302.
6. MENDONÇA, *O celeste porvir,* p. 64.
7. MENDONÇA, *O celeste porvir,* p. 66.
8. BOSCH, *Missão transformadora,* p. 310.
9. NEILL, *História das missões,* p. 242.
10. GONZÁLEZ, *Uma história do pensamento cristão,* p. 224.
11. GONZÁLEZ, *Uma história do pensamento cristão,* p. 213.
12. BOSCH, *Missão transformadora,* p. 318.
13. GONZÁLEZ, *Uma história do pensamento cristão,* p. 213.
14. MENDONÇA, *O celeste porvir,* p. 107.
15. BOSCH, *Missão transformadora,* p. 328.
16. 19th Century and Voluntarism – Bosch says that at the end of this century and the beginning of the 20th century, there was an explosion in the creation of agencies and protestant missionary organizations, offering various opportunities for young people, students and people who felt "called" to go around the world to preach the gospel.
17. MENDONÇA, *O celeste porvir,* p. 89.
18. Slavery and civil war – the question of slavery is interwoven with the North-American conquests which took land from Mexico, and with a southern economy

which depended on the work of slaves. The North was opposed to such ideas, and the opposition culminated in the civil war.

19. BOSCH, *Missão transformadora,* p. 344.
20. See "Vocação ao fundamentalismo; introdução ao espírito do protestantismo de missão no Brasil". In: MENDONÇA, Antonio G. and VELASQUES, Prócoro. *Introdução ao protestantismo no Brasil.* São Paulo: Edições Loyola, 1990. Mendonça refers to this text, saying that it defines the fundamental elements for a "sound doctrine." He comments that the fundamentalists generally identify themselves as "conservative evangelical", not admitting that they are fundamentalists.
21. BOSCH, *Missão transformadora,* p. 280.
22. LÉONARD, Émile. *O protestanismo brasileiro.* São Paulo: ASTE, 2002, p. 84.
23. PRADO, Eduardo. *A ilusão americana. [The American Illusion]*. São Paulo: IBRASA, 1980. p. 61.
24. PIEDRA, Arturo. *Evangelização protestante na América Latina; análise das razões que justificaram e promoveram a expansão protestante (1860-1960). [Protestant evangelization in Latin America; an analysis of the reasons which justified and promoted protestant expansion (1830-1960).]* São Leopoldo: Sinodal / CLAI, 2006. p. 30.
25. PIEDRA, *Evangelização protestante na América Latina,* p. 37.
26. PIEDRA, *Evangelização protestante na América Latina,* p. 37.
27. Manifest Destiny – A belief rooted in the sense of the superiority of the West with the strong tendency to treat people from other cultures as inferior and which reached its maximum expression in the colonial expansion of the West, mainly in the period between 1880 and 1920. England had ideas of the superiority of Protestantism in relation to Catholicism. The United States embraced the idea and believed that because of their qualities, God had chosen them to be his representatives amongst the other peoples of the world.
28. BOSCH, *Missão transformadora,* p. 375.
29. GONZALEZ, Justo L. *História Ilustrada do cristianismo; a era dos novos horizontes. [Illustrated History of Christianity: the era of new horizons]*. São Paulo: Edições Vida Nova. 1981. p. 41.
30. PIEDRA, *Evangelização protestante na América Latina,* p. 42.
31. MENDONÇA, *O celeste porvir,* p. 75.
32. MENDONÇA, *O celeste porvir,* p. 94.
33. MENDONÇA, *O celeste porvir,* p. 95.
34. BOSCH, *Missão transformadora,* p. 360.
35. MENDONÇA, *O celeste porvir,* p. 101.
36. LÉVI-STRAUSS, Claude. *Raça e história. [Race and History]*. Queluz de Baixo, Portugal: Presença, 2010. p. 64.
37. CÉSAR, Elben M. Lenz. *História da evangelização do Brasil; dos jesuítas aos neopentecostais.* Viçosa: Ultimato, 2000. p. 14.
38. The first Methodist missionary who arrived in Brazil was Rev. Fountain E. Pitts, in 1835, but Daniel Kidder became more famous. He arrived in 1837 and left many impressions by the distribution of Bibles in Brazil and also by his book *Reminiscências de Viagens e Permanências nas Províncias do Sul to Brasil.*
39. Civil War – Conflict in the United States which began on 12th April, 1861 and ended on 9th April 1865, basically "economic interests between the North, which had grown in industry, and the South, which was principally agricultural" (DE OLIVEIRA, Betty Antunes. *Centelha em restolho seco; a contribuição para a história dos primórdios do trabalho batista no Brasil. [Spark in dry stubble: a*

contribution to the history of the beginning of Baptist work in Brazil.] São Paulo: Edições Vida Nova, 2005. p. 27.

40. OLIVEIRA, *Centelha em restolho seco,* p. 352.
41. MENDONÇA, *O celeste porvir,* p. 162.
42. MENDONÇA, *O celeste porvir,* p. 163.
43. BOSCH, *Missão transformadora,* p. 366.
44. PEREIRA, José dos Reis. *História dos batistas no Brasil.* Rio de Janeiro: JUERP: 1972. p. 172.
45. Pérola Byington was from a Baptist family who emigrated with a group of confederates from the USA to Santa Bárbara (in Brazil) and who died in 1963. OLIVEIRA, *Centelha em restolho seco,* pp 351 and 360.
46. MENDONÇA, *O celeste porvir,* p. 298.
47. MILLER, Darrow L. *Vocação: escreva sua assinatura no Universo.* [*Vocation: write your membership in the Universe*] Instituto e Publicações Transforma / DNA Brasil, 2012, p. 68.
48. ESCOBAR, Samuel. "Missiologia evangélica; olhando para o futuro na virada do século". [Evangelical missiology; looking to the future at the turn of the century]. In: *Missiologia global para o século XXI; the Foz do Iguaçu Consultation.* Londrina: Descoberta, 2001. p. 155.
49. BOSCH, *Missão transformadora,* p. 413.
50. JENKINS, Philip. *A próxima cristandade; a chegada do cristianismo global.* Rio de Janeiro: Record, 2004. p. 150. [cf Philip Jenkins, *The Next Christendom: the coming of global Christianity.* Oxford: Oxford University Press, 2004.]

Chapter Four

1. BOSCH, David. *Missão transformadora; mudanças de paradigma na teologia da missão.* São Leopoldo: Sinodal, 2002. p. 366. [cf David J. Bosch, *Transforming Mission, Paradigm Shifts in Theology of Mission,* Orbis Books, New York, 1991.]
2. BOSCH, *Missão transformadora,* p. 378.
3. SANTOS, Boaventura de Sousa. *Semear outras soluções; os caminhos da biodiversidade e dos conhecimentos rivais.* Rio de Janeiro: Civilização Brasileira, 2005. p. 28.
4. Acculturation – "the fusion of two different cultures which, entering into continuous contact, begin changes in the norms of the culture of both of them" (MARCONI, Marina; PRESOTTO, Zelia M. *Antropologia; uma introdução.* [*Anthropology: an introduction*] São Paulo: Atlas. 2001, p. 65.
5. SONG, Choan Seng. "The Church is God's partner in re-creation". *Theologies and Cultures,* 5(22), (December 2008). Taiwan: University & Tainan Thelogical College, 2008. p. 111.
6. PADILLA, René, *O futuro do Movimento de Lausanne.* p. 3. [This article was published in English, in the International Bulletin of Mission Research, 35(2), (Apr. 2011), pp. 86-87,.]
7. SANTOS, *Semear outras soluções,* p. 94.
8. Coloniality – "Refers to the logical structure of colonial domination," whilst colonialism refers; to a historical period. MIGNOLO, Walter. *The Idea of Latin America.* Malden, MA: Blackwell Publishing, 2005. p. 7.
9. SANTOS, Boaventura de Sousa, *Renovar a teoria crítica e reinventar a emancipação social,* [*Renew critical theory and reinvent social emancipation,*] São Paulo: Boitempo, 2007. p. 59.

10. LAPLANTINE, François. *Aprender antropologia.* [*Learning anthropology.*] São Paulo: Brasiliense, 1991. p. 52.

11. Sul – for Boaventura de Sousa Santos, this "Sul" ("South") refers to a sociological category and not necessarily to a geographical position, p. 23.

12. 1 Corinthians 13:1-3.

13. John 20:12.

14. Matthew 22:93; 7:12.

15. FREIRE, Paulo. *Pedagogia da autonomia; saberes necessários à prática educativa.* (*Pedagogy of Autonomy: necessary for educative practice*) São Paulo: Paz e Terra, 1997, p. 135.

16. WIRTH, Lauro Emilio. "O universalismo missionário dos cristãoes e o colonialismo; uma visão a partir da história do cristianismo". [The missionary universalism of Christians and colonialism; a vision from the history of Christianity.] In: *Missão e educação teológica.* São Paulo: ASTE, 2011. p. 58.

17. QUIJANO, Anibal. "Coloniality of power, eurocentrism and social classification". In: *Coloniality at Large: Latin America and the postcolonial debate.* Durham, NC / London: Duke University Press, 2008. p. 192.

18. MIGNOLO, Walter. *The Idea of Latin America.* Malden, MA: Blackwell Publishing, 2005, p. 9. [cf The Idea of Latin America, Wiley Blackwell Manifestos, 2005.]

19. *Descrioulização* – In Angola, in the 1950's, measures were taken to "whiten" the cities. The black people were pushed out of the great urban centres into *musseques* [sandy plots of land on the outskirts of Luanda, occupied by poor people.]

20. SCHUBERT, Benedict. *A Guerra e as igrejas; Angola 1961 – 1991.* (The War and the Churches) Basel, Switzerland: P. Schlettwein Publishing. 2000. p. 43.

21. CHIMBINDA, Jorge Simeão Ferreira. *O nome na identidade Umbundu; contributo antropológico.* Huambo: Estudos da Tradição Umbundu, 2009. p. 24.

22. UNESCO. *Convenção sobre a proteção e promoção de diversidade das expressões culturais.* Capítulo 1, artigo 1°, item 'c'. Paris: Unesco Brasilia Office, Representação da Unesco no Brasil, 2005.

23. CHANDA, Nayan. *Sem fronteiras; os comerciantes, missionários, adventureiros e soldados que moldaram a globalização.* [*Without Frontiers: the merchants, missisonaries, adventurers and soldiers who shaped globalization.*] Rio de Janeiro: Record, 2011. p. 172.

24. Titus 1:16.

25. DRC – Dutch Reformed Church – *Afrikaans* tradition in South Africa.

26. YATES, Timothy. David Bosch: "South African context, universal missiology: ecclesiology in the emerging missionary paradigm". *International Bulletin of Missionary Research*, 2009. p. 73.

27. See my dissertation for my Masters Degree "Crise e Esperança; a praxis pastoral da igreja batista na Guerra de Angola". Universidade Metodista de São Paulo, 2005.

28. SILVA, Jarbas Ferreira and NASCIMENTO Analzira. Missão, *Missões antimissão; o projeto de Deus e os empreendimentos humanos.* São Paulo: Editora Reflexão, 2011. p. 205.

29. KREGNESS, Curtis A. *África, amor e dor; uma mulher responde a Castro Alves.* São Paulo: Edições Vida Nova, 2005. p. 26.

30. Marcelo and Elaine Okasawara are missionaries of the National Missions Board of the Brazilian Baptist Convention. The conversation occurred in the Água Branca Baptist Church, on December 26th, 2012, in a meeting to evaluate the partnership.

31. HUMMES, Claudio. *Transição da igreja.* Interview for the *Folha de São Paulo* [newspaper], March 16th, 2013.

32. HOORNAERT, Eduardo. *História da igreja no Brasil; ensaio de interpretação a partir do povo.* [*History of the Church in Brasil: an interpretive essay beginning with the people.*] Petrópolis: Vozes, 1992. p. 117.
33. BOSCH, *Missão transformadora,* p. 434.
34. BOSCH, *Missão transformadora,* p. 17.
35. BOSCH, *Missão transformadora,* p. 469.
36. Matthew 28:19-20.
37. LIBANIO, João Batista. *A religião no início do milênio.* [*Religion at the Beginning of the Millennium.*] São Paulo: Edições Loyola, 2002. p. 136.
38. FREIRE, Paulo. *Pedagogia do oprimido.* Sao Paulo: Paz e Terra, 2007. p. 98. [cf Paulo Freire, *Pedagogy of the Oppressed.* New York: Continuum, 2007.]
39. MOVIMENTO LAUSANNE. *O compromissio da Cidade do Cabo; uma declaração de fé e um chamado para agir.* [*The city of Cape Town commitment: a declaration of faith and a call to action*] Curitiba / Viçosa: MG: Encontro Publicações / Editora UItimato, 2011. p. 68. (The Cape Town Declaration is available online at: www.lausanne.org/ctcommitment).
40. MOVIMENTO LAUSANNE. *O compromissio da Cidade do Cabo,* p. 17.
41. ESCOBAR, Samuel. "Missiologia evangélica; olhando para o futuro na virada do século". [Evangelical Missiology: looking to the future at the turn of the century]. In: TAYLOR, William D., Ed. *Missiologia global para o século XXI; a consulta de Foz do Iguaçu.* [*Global missiology for the XXI century; the Foz do Iguaçu consultation*] Londrina: Descoberta, 2001. p. 150.
42. John 20:12.
43. COMBLIN, José. *O Espírito Santo e a tradição de Jesus.* São Paulo: Nhanduti, 2012. p. 102.
44. ZWETSCH, Roberto E. *Missão como com-paixão; por uma teologia da missão em perspectiva latino-americana.* [*Mission as 'with-passion': towards a theology of mission from the Latin American perspective.*] São Leopoldo / Quito: Sinodal / CLAI, 2008. p. 91.
45. Igreja Batista de Água Branca, in São Paulo, which develops four social missionary projects in communities with a low HDI [human development index] in different regions of Brazil and maintains partnerships with 32 organizations through the IBAB Solidarity Network.
46. SILVA, Jarbas Ferreira and NASCIMENTO, Analzira. *Missão, missões, antimissão; o projeto de Deus e os empreendimentos humanos.* [*Mission, missions, anti-mission; God's project and human enterprises.*] São Paulo: Editora Reflexão, 2011. p. 202.
47. BOSCH, *Missão transformadora,* p. 11.
48. TODOROV, Tzvestan, *A conquisa da América; a questão do outro.* São Paulo: Martins Fontes, 2003. p. 364. [cf *The conquest of America: the question of the Other.* New York: Harper Row. 1984.]
49. GREENWOOD, Philip J. *Fazedores-de-tendas – fazedores de discípulos; a preparação e a capacitação dos fazedores-de-tendas brasileiros.* [*Tent-makers – disciple-makers: preparation and training of Brazilian tent-makers.*] Londrina: Descoberta, 2005. p. 98.
50. MULLER, Roland. *O mensageiro, a mensagem; a comunidade; três questões fundamentais para um plantador de igrejas transculturais.* Atibaia: Editora Prega a Palavra, 2013. p. 323. [cf *The Messenger, The Message, and the Community: Three Critical Issues for the Cross-cultural Church-Planter.* Roland Muller Books, 2015.]
51. SUNG, Jung Mo. *Educar para reencantar a vida.* [*Educate to re-enchant life*]. Petrópolis: Vozes, 2006. p.128.

Conclusion

1. SANTOS, Boaventura de Sousa. *Renovar a teoria crítica e reinventar a emancipação social.* São Paulo: Boitempo, 2007. P. 55.
2. FREIRE, Paulo. *Pedagogia do oprimido.* São Paulo: Paz e Terra, 2007. p. 173.
3. GREENWOOD, Philip J. *Fazedores-de-tendas – fazedores de discípulos; a preparação e capacitação dos fazerdores-de-tendas brasileiros.* Londrina: Descoberta, 2005. p. 98.
4. www.indigenas.org.br. *Quais são as principais razões que impedem a igreja brasileira de enviar mais missionários tranculturais.* p. 2.
5. BOSCH, David. *Missão transformadora, mudanças de paradigma na teologia da missão.* São Leopoldo: Sinodal, 2002. p. 609.
6. LÉONARD, Émile. *O protestantismo brasileiro.* São Paulo: ASTE, 2002. p. 35